"Joseph Luna's book is an invaluable aid to policy professionals, academics and development planning practitioners to understand the problem of public policy and corruption. It is evidence-based and combines empirical knowledge with in-depth theoretical and historical knowledge. It is a required reading for academics, policy makers as well as students."

— *Kwame A. Ninsin, Emeritus Professor of Political Science, University of Ghana*

"This is an exceptional contribution to the study of political financing. Luna unpicks the dynamic interactions among key players with impressive analytical precision, deftly applying game theory and collective action models to examine his cases. He tells a story that will resonate with scholars of political corruption and clientelism everywhere, yet also illuminates several features of low-resource contexts which amplify the usual pressures on political actors. The book is also a gripping read, fluently written and rich with the personalities and narratives of the protagonists."

— *Elizabeth Dávid-Barrett, Senior Lecturer in Politics and Director of the Centre for the Study of Corruption, University of Sussex, UK*

I0128902

Political Financing
in Developing Countries

This book argues that to fully grasp the decision-making of politicians and political actors in developing countries, we must first understand how politicians finance their campaigns for office—and to whom they are indebted and expected to repay.

Political Financing in Developing Countries focuses on Ghana in depth, a country often held up as an example of a successful, two-party democracy with regular party changes in government. However, it is unlikely that candidates and political parties are wealthy enough to finance the increasing costs of campaigns and constituent demands, and successful democratic outcomes could be masking a system that actually hinders development progress. Drawing on nearly 200 interviews and extensive fieldwork, this book posits that political funds are extracted by an iron square of politicians, bureaucrats, construction contractors, and political-party chairs which rigs the procurement of local-development projects to generate kickbacks. The iron square remains robust across party changes in government due to reciprocity obligations that minimize contractors' income risks. Ultimately, this web of kickbacks diminishes the quality of development by reducing the funds available for projects and distorting incentives to monitor projects. To break this iron square, the book recommends replacing sealed-bid procurement—a "best practice" that ignores on-the-ground realities—with a system that accounts for income stabilization and social obligations.

Overall, the book argues that scholars of development should advance research on political finance to identify and then alleviate the games that decision makers must play to survive in the political sphere. *Political Financing in Developing Countries* will be an important and timely resource for scholars across development studies, politics, economics, and African Studies.

Joseph Luna is an Economist at the John A. Volpe National Transportation Systems Center, USA. He holds a PhD in Government from Harvard University and has advised international-development projects in South Asia and Sub-Saharan Africa.

Routledge Explorations in Development Studies

This Development Studies series features innovative and original research at the regional and global scale. It promotes interdisciplinary scholarly works drawing on a wide spectrum of subject areas, in particular politics, health, economics, rural and urban studies, sociology, environment, anthropology, and conflict studies.

Topics of particular interest are globalization; emerging powers; children and youth; cities; education; media and communication; technology development; and climate change.

In terms of theory and method, rather than basing itself on any orthodoxy, the series draws broadly on the tool kit of the social sciences in general, emphasizing comparison, the analysis of the structure and processes, and the application of qualitative and quantitative methods.

The Power of Civil Society in the Middle East and North Africa
Peace-building, Change, and Development
Edited by Ibrahim Natil, Chiara Pierobon, and Lilian Tauber

Global Business Cycles and Developing Countries
Eri Ikeda

Practices of Citizenship in East Africa
Perspectives from Philosophical Pragmatism
Edited by Katariina Holma and Tiina Kontinen

Political Financing in Developing Countries
A Case from Ghana
Joseph Luna

For more information about this series, please visit: https://www.routledge.com

Political Financing
in Developing Countries
A Case from Ghana

Joseph Luna

Routledge
Taylor & Francis Group

LONDON AND NEW YORK

First published 2020
by Routledge
2 Park Square, Milton Park, Abingdon, Oxon OX14 4RN

and by Routledge
52 Vanderbilt Avenue, New York, NY 10017

Routledge is an imprint of the Taylor & Francis Group, an informa business

First issued in paperback 2021

British Library Cataloguing-in-Publication Data
A catalogue record for this book is available from the British Library

Library of Congress Cataloging-in-Publication Data
Names: Luna, Joseph, author.
Title: Political financing in developing countries:
a case from Ghana / Joseph Luna.
Description: Abingdon, Oxon; New York, NY: Routledge, 2020. |
Includes bibliographical references and index.
Identifiers: LCCN 2019036244 (print) | LCCN 2019036245 (ebook) |
ISBN 9780367429560 (hardback) | ISBN 9781003000372 (ebook)
Subjects: LCSH: Campaign funds—Ghana. | Campaign funds—Corrupt
practices—Ghana. | Politics, Practical—Ghana. |
Ghana—Politics and government—2001–
Classification: LCC JQ3039.A3 L86 2020 (print) |
LCC JQ3039.A3 (ebook) | DDC 324.7809667—dc23
LC record available at https://lccn.loc.gov/2019036244
LC ebook record available at https://lccn.loc.gov/2019036245

ISBN: 978-0-367-42956-0 (hbk)
ISBN: 978-1-03-208596-8 (pbk)
ISBN: 978-1-003-00037-2 (ebk)

Typeset in Times New Roman
by codeMantra

Copyright Page Disclaimer
"The views expressed in this book are solely the author's own,
and do not necessarily represent those of the Volpe Center,
U.S. Department of Transportation, or the United States".

Contents

Illustrations

Figures

Tables

Acknowledgments

I am lucky to have benefited from the kindness and support of so many. At Harvard, I am deeply grateful to my dissertation committee for guiding and broadening my intellectual pursuits: Robert Bates, Daniel Carpenter, Arthur Spirling, and Lucie White. Bob has been a mentor to me since my undergraduate days, and his example has truly shaped how I think.

In preparing this book for publication, I would like to thank Helena Hurd, Leila Walker, and the team at Routledge for believing in this project and helping me throughout the process. I also greatly appreciate the comments from two anonymous reviewers, which helped to strengthen this work.

I would not have gotten to where I am today without the love and support of my family. My parents, Jose and Victoria Luna, have always believed in me and worked tirelessly to give me a better life. I am humbled by what they have sacrificed for me. My wife, Michelle Storch, has believed in this project since meeting me, and I could not have finished it without her love and encouragement. I am truly lucky to share a life with her.

This book was made by the stories of countless Ghanaian public servants. Since my first visit to Ghana in 2008, I have learned so much and have always felt welcome. For their friendship and hospitality, I would like to particularly thank Elionai Adu-Labi, Eric Tetteh, and Siisi Ocran. I am grateful to Akuamoah Ofosu-Boateng, Alhaji Ishaq, Cofie Agama, Joseph Dasanah, Karl Arhin, and Kwadwo Antwi Adjei for their patience and assistance with my research.

To the nearly 200 politicians, bureaucrats, contractors, party officials, chiefs, and opinion leaders interviewed for this book, thank you for sharing your stories. I was amazed by the fervent commitment so many of you displayed to developing Ghana—and frustrated to learn of the challenges you each faced in trying to carry out that mandate. I hope that one day those challenges can be alleviated. This book is for you and all those who do their best to serve the public.

Abbreviations

DACF	District Assemblies Common Fund
DBO	District Budget Officer
DCD	District Coordinating Director
DCE	District Chief Executive
DDF	District Development Facility
DFID	Department for International Development
DPO	District Planning Officer
EPA	Everyday Political Analysis
MP	Member of Parliament
NDC	National Democratic Congress
NGO	Non-Governmental Organization
NP	Non-Performing
NPP	New Patriotic Party
OECD-DAC	Organisation for Economic Cooperation and Development, Development Assistance Committee
PEA	Political-Economy Analysis
RM	Regional Minister
SIDA	Swedish International Development Cooperation Agency
USAID	United States Agency for International Development

Introduction
Two puzzles in politics

The financing of politics shapes a country's economic and social situation. In democratic countries, citizens have the opportunity to influence local and national policies, but those citizens must win elections and become politicians to implement those policies. However, winning elections is not straightforward. A candidate must create campaign messages that are distinct from her opponents—and find a way to convince enough voters to accept these messages and vote the candidate into office. Unless that candidate is exceedingly wealthy, she must turn to others to finance her campaign. For those who invest in a candidate, it is sensible that many of them desire a return on their investment. Financiers expect to have some influence over the candidate's agenda should she win office. The candidate-politician must now temper her initial expectations and work to "repay" those who helped her win: in other words, whom a politician owes, defines how she will behave. These multiplying demands crowd out a politician's initial agenda, and if she does not meet those demands, she runs the risk of losing essential support for the next election.

It is critical for political-economy analysts in international development to understand the processes and consequences of political finance. Upon reaching office, the politician cannot become an island, solely pursuing her own agenda. She is not free of her debts. She operates in a larger "political ecosystem" that helps (and hinders) her in implementing her desired policies. That political ecosystem includes bureaucrats, private businesses (for instance, construction contractors), and the leadership of political parties. To win an election, a candidate-politician must have a good relationship with political-party leadership, who can garner additional support for her. Once in office, the politician's proposed policies would be written by bureaucrats and given their stamp of expertise. These policies may then be implemented directly by the bureaucracy, or, in the case of club and public goods, they are implemented by a private contractor selected—ostensibly—through public procurement.

In a well-functioning democratic country, political-bureaucratic processes are relatively efficient and often invisible; however, in many developing countries, these processes do not work well and the resulting outcomes can be detrimental to economic and social development. Many developing countries do not have long-standing traditions of transparent elections or procurement. This book, drawing from extensive fieldwork in Ghana, argues that the key players in a developing country's political ecosystem are connected—and influenced—by that country's system of political financing. Bureaucrats' social standing and long-term savings are closely connected to political sources of money. Contractors collude with politicians and bureaucrats to guarantee that they win contracts, even if they lack the appropriate qualifications. Despite lofty political promises to improve conditions, many developing countries continue to demonstrate poor economic and social outcomes as a result of these connections to political financing.

Though political finance shapes—even sustains—the political ecosystem in a developing country, we are left with two puzzles concerning the financing of politics. **First, where does the money to finance political campaigns actually come from?** We observe in many countries that candidates erect numerous billboards, travel the country, and create advertisements for radio, television, and social media. Candidates employ growing numbers of staff, replete with vehicles and outreach operations. Candidates also engage in vote buying and the purchase of gifts for party loyalists. However, it is unlikely, given how poor many voters are, that candidates and parties raise enough funding from party dues and voter contributions. It is likely that such funds come from questionable sources, possibly via illegal means. This question is additionally important in that many developing countries have adopted such democratic institutions as local elections from other countries, but with little guidance on the funding of campaigns. It is not clear that such institutions and the funding of campaigns are strongly rooted in a given country's social norms. **The second puzzle: despite poor development outcomes and regular changes in government, how does this political-financing situation persist?** Many politicians and bureaucrats know that their actions could be improved to yield better economic and social outcomes, and they also know that many examples of improved governance exist around the world. Even more puzzling, Ghana, the focus of this book, has a first-past-the-post electoral system, which yields two major political parties and regular party changes in government. With the opposition party locked out of lucrative ministries and local governments, why has a governing party not been able to permanently crowd out the opposition? What motivates the political ecosystem to maintain the *status quo*?

Motivations

Political-economy analysis (PEA) in international development must be rooted in an understanding of the motivations of politicians and associated political actors, including bureaucrats, construction contractors, and political-party leaders.[1] These people make the decisions that can cause a development project to succeed or fail. While scholarly perspectives on these actors' motivations are presented in turn, it is critical to note that none of these actors exist in isolation: they are each influenced by formal and informal rules as well as by the actions of each other (Hudson, Marquette, & Waldock 2016; Baez Camargo & Koechlin 2018).

Politicians

For politicians, many scholars argue that their actions are motivated by a desire to win elections (Mayhew 1974; Fenno 1978). To win these elections, politicians engage in credit claiming and position taking during their campaigns (Mayhew 1974).[2] However, political motivations are nuanced and embedded in other social structures (Schlesinger 1966; Fenno 1990). As Schlesinger (1966) encapsulates in the American case,

> Since the politician is also always a citizen, it is never possible to abstract him as pure officeseeker, in the same degree to which we can isolate the businessman or the doctor. The politician's other interests are always involved in his decisions as politician.

A politician's current behavior in office may be molded by expected future employment in the private sector or other economic or political interests (Schlesinger 1966; Lessig 2011; Schneer & Palmer 2016). Empirical studies have demonstrated that politicians are more likely to pay attention to constituents who are their campaign financiers (e.g., business owners, union leaders) compared to constituents who did not contribute to a politician's campaigns (Kalla & Broockman 2015). Powell (2014) demonstrates that campaign contributions can increase lobbyists' access to state legislators in the US. In the UK, the Labour Party's historically close financial relationship with trade unions has fostered allegations of unions' excessive influence in party politics (Power 2016). Both the Labour and Conservative parties allow for privileged access to those who donate above certain thresholds; such access can be popularly perceived as having influence over political processes (Power 2018). These "other interests" can influence how the politician campaigns and acts while in office—and what she might expect upon leaving office.

In developing countries, there can be a multitude of other interests and factors that affect how a politician acts during a campaign and while in office. Scholars have demonstrated that, under certain conditions, politicians favor constituents from the same ethnicity (Posner 2005; Ichino & Nathan 2013) and provide private goods to potential voters (van de Walle 2007; Lindberg 2010). These political incentives are underlined by additional factors, such as the historical development of institutions (Acemoglu, Johnson, & Robinson 2001). This book does not argue that political incentives are necessarily more complex or difficult in developing countries compared to other countries—the incentives may differ, but politicians must still consider them during the course of their campaigns and time in office.

Bureaucrats

While politicians may set policy directions, these policies are ultimately formalized and implemented by bureaucracies. Weber (1922) describes the ideal bureaucracy as a rational, legal institution comprised of specialized administrative experts. Weber's bureaucracy is characterized by merit recruitment, hierarchy, uniformity, impersonality, and political neutrality. Looking within the bureaucracy, Downs (1967) discusses five typologies of bureaucrats: climbers, conservers, zealots, advocates, and statesmen. Climbers seek power, income, and prestige, while conservers seek to maintain their holds on these attributes. Zealots, advocates, and statesmen are more altruistic, showing various degrees of devotion to issues and broader programs. Similar to other professionals, bureaucrats devote attention to promotion, and the actions they undertake to earn promotions impact policy outcomes (Lipsky 1980). Bureaucrats often must also meet professional criteria that are determined by outside associations, particularly if they are considering careers outside the bureaucracy (Kaufman 1960; Skowronek 1982; Alesina & Tabellini 2007). Beyond career considerations, a bureaucracy's history, culture, and norms also determine how these officials approach tasks (Kaufman 1960; Wilson 1989). External environments, however, can allow enterprising bureaucrats to reshape an agency's outputs. Carpenter (2001) demonstrates that mid-level bureaucrats of the United States Postal Service and the United States Forest Service coordinated support from outside their agencies to implement their preferred policies against political opposition.

In many countries, bureaucratic positions are respected pathways to political and private success (Johnson 1982; Woodall 1996); however, bureaucratic incentives and actions can differ in developing countries. For many African citizens, traditional and family-based demands encourage talented and educated young people to pursue a career in the civil service to ensure that they can provide benefits to these family members (Achebe 1960). Ekeh (1975) distinguishes between a bureaucrat's official and personal obligations, highlighting the influence of family demands on how a bureaucrat carries out her duties. Price (1975), surveying potential civil servants training at the University of Ghana, indicates that family and social pressures are high for civil servants.

Recent scholarship has employed quantitative and experimental methods to yield new insights into bureaucratic behavior in developing countries. Gingerich (2013) finds that some South American bureaucrats conduct corrupt activities for political parties to position themselves for lucrative political careers. Focusing on India, Hanna and Wang (2017) employ a laboratory experiment to analyze selection motivations of students seeking entry to the India Civil Service. These authors find that students who cheat on the laboratory experiment are more likely to seek entry to the India Civil Service, implying that they will engage in corrupt acts in the future. In a landmark study, Rasul and Rogger (2018) surveyed thousands of Nigerian civil servants to determine the effects of management practices on bureaucratic performance. While their results indicate that increased autonomy for Nigerian civil servants can lead to better outcomes on smaller projects, the authors caution against importing incentives/ monitoring practices, which may negatively affect bureaucratic outcomes. Incentives and monitoring practices may fail because bureaucrats work in "multi-tasking environments", where bureaucrats conduct other efforts that are not related to project completion. As such, incentives and monitoring might actually burden bureaucrats with more regulation (Rasul & Rogger 2018). Focusing on Ghana, Rasul et al. (2018) find similar results, where greater autonomy leads to better bureaucratic outcomes, while increasing incentives and monitoring has the opposite effect. Similarly, with respect to autonomy in the Ghanaian bureaucracy, Brierley (2019a) demonstrates that politicians' threats of political transfer can incentivize bureaucrats to extract state resources.

Contractors

Unlike politicians and bureaucrats, private construction contractors are not well studied in the political economy of development. Blundo and Olivier de Sardan's (2006) ethnography of local contractors in Francophone West Africa is a rare example, and the authors argue that contractors are connected with politicians and collude to win contracts. Woodall (1996), studying the Japanese case, finds extensive collusion between politicians, elite bureaucrats, and construction firms. Contractors are critical actors in a developing country. They are the ones who actually build the development projects citizens demand. Contractors, as the recipients and executors of government-funded development projects, are the synapse across which public funds can enter private pockets. Certainly not all contractors are thinking of political influence when they start in the industry, but many turn to political favor to ensure stable profits. Stable profits are likely the chief incentive for most contractors in developing countries. In Ghana, one does not need special training to be a contractor, and the groups assigned to monitor contractors rarely enforce regulations. Being a contractor and having the right connections can be an immediate path to wealth and influence.

Party leaders

Local party leaders (chairs) connect the politicians and the masses, and they wield influence over politicians' futures. In my observation of Ghana, party chairs are coordinators and information conduits for the three players described above. Party chairs head the system that turns out the votes for political candidates, and they essentially oversee the primaries that select candidates. Cases drawn from the political history of the US demonstrate how party leaders raised funds and turned out votes. These cases are particularly relevant for studying political finance in Ghana because they illustrate such themes as ethnic politics, graft, norms of reciprocity, and the highly personal connections between chairs and their constituents. At many points, these American political machines centered on influential, individual chairs who, from the background and oftentimes free from prosecution, manipulated political activities. Riordon's (1905) description of a Tammany Hall official, George Washington Plunkitt, approximates characteristics of party machinery and chairs in Ghana, such as casual acceptance of patronage appointments and graft. Similarly, Royko's (1971) biography of Chicago mayor Richard J. Daley—who was also chair of the Cook County Democratic Party—details Daley's embrace of machine politics, patronage, and ethnic divisions.

Though such party chairs have accumulated power, wealth, and influence, many have the core desire to care for constituents, especially those who support the party.[3] Party loyalists in Ghana, commonly known as foot soldiers, often expect party leaders to provide them with jobs. For Ghanaian party chairs, these jobs can be found in civil-service positions (Sigman 2015; Brierley 2019b), but they are also easily generated in the construction industry through the preferential awarding of contracts—from which party leaders can skim some "honest graft" (Riordon 1905). Sigman (2015) finds that, at the elite level in Ghana, party leaders reward loyalists with key government positions, thus enabling continued access to state resources for party financing. Unlike politicians, though, party chairs and their activities are not at the front of the stage. They operate behind the scenes, mustering the money and votes needed to ensure a political victory.

Implications for donors

As detailed above, the motivations of political actors are complex. Nonetheless, understanding these motivations and local contexts can advance how donors conduct PEA and improve the success of development projects. Leftwich (2007) argues that development outcomes are politically determined, and practitioners should distinguish between the "rules of the game" and the "games within the rules". Carothers and de Gramont (2013) note that, while donors have made significant strides over the past few decades in bolstering PEA, they have not fully incorporated PEA-driven goals and methods into their socioeconomic sectors—a phenomenon that these authors term, an "almost revolution". Toeba (2018) argues that affluent countries, which are anchored in neoliberal economic theories, affect anti-corruption and procurement policies in such countries as Lesotho; these policies are not tailored to their local contexts and ultimately fail. Jakupec and Kelly (2019) emphasize the need for Western donors to improve the theoretical grounding of their PEA work, given the appeal of alternative development models and the rise of populist politics in donor countries. Indeed, this book engages with populist rhetoric espoused by such politicians as Bernie Sanders through its focus on connecting political finance with politicians' behavior. With respect to political-finance regulations, Norris and Abel van Es (2016) examine disclosure requirements, contribution limits, spending caps, and public subsidies across multiple cases in both developed and developing countries. Such policies are often lauded as "best practices", but the authors concede that solutions to corruption associated with political finance need to be rooted in local contexts and norms. While it is important to understand the macro-political and regulatory contexts that shape political motivations in developing countries, this book advances those broad approaches by investigating a specific institution, political financing, in depth.

For their part, many donors have incorporated PEA into their development practices—the "almost revolution" notwithstanding. The Organisation for Economic Cooperation and Development's Development Assistance Committee (OECD-DAC) provides the following definition for PEA:

> Political economy analysis is concerned with the interaction of political and economic processes in a society: the distribution of power and wealth between different groups and individuals, and the processes that create, sustain, and transform these relationships over time.
>
> (Department for International Development 2009)

Donors have interpreted and operationalized this definition in a variety of ways. The Department for International Development's (DFID) approach to PEA is concerned with the interests and incentives facing different groups in society; the role that formal institutions and informal norms play in shaping human interaction and political-economic competition; and the impact values and ideas, including political ideologies, religion, and cultural beliefs, have on political behavior and public policy (DFID 2009).

To operationalize PEA, DFID applies its "Drivers of Change" approach to three areas, working from the broadest to the most specific: country-level analysis, sector-level analysis, and problem-driven analysis. The key question of interest of this approach is "how policy and institutional reforms that benefit poor people emerge and endure, and why in many cases they are blocked" (DFID 2009). At the country level, the goal is to find which drivers of change will shape incentives for change over the short-, medium-, and long-term. At the sector level, stakeholder maps are created so that analysts can identify influential actors, key interests, and incentives, and how these actors and incentives shape the overall sector and potential reforms. Lastly, in problem-driven analysis, development practitioners identify the problem, issue, or vulnerability to be addressed; map out the institutional and governance weaknesses that sustain the given problem; and investigate down to the political-economy root causes that constrain change (DFID 2009). DFID's (2009) framework draws on practices from a variety of other donors, including the Swedish International Development Cooperation Agency (SIDA), the Netherlands Ministry of Foreign Affairs, and the World Bank (DFID 2009). United States Agency for International Development (USAID 2018) applies a PEA framework that embraces "thinking and working politically", and draws much inspiration from DFID's (2009) framework.[4]

For many PEA practitioners, the approaches outlined by DFID (2009) and other donors may be overly complex, resource intensive, and difficult to explain to non-PEA practitioners. There may be sizeable gaps in country-specific political-economy knowledge that could significantly extend budgets and timelines. Hudson, Marquette, and Waldock (2016) offer a simplified framework called "Everyday Political Analysis" (EPA). This framework specifies that practitioners should shift their focus from the recipients of a potential program to those who are powerful (e.g., decision makers) in the given context (Hudson, Marquette, & Waldock 2016). Under EPA, there are two steps: understanding interests (what do people think?) and understanding change (what space and capacity do people have to effect change?). Under each of these steps are a series of yes/no questions:

- Step 1: Understanding interests
  - Is what they want clear?
  - Are they acting in line with their core beliefs?
  - Do you understand the constraints they face?
  - Is it clear who and what the key influences on them are?
  - Is their behavior being shaped by social norms about what is appropriate?

- Step 2: Understanding change
  - Are they the key decision maker?
  - Do they have potential coalition partners?
  - Are their decision points clear?
  - Is their framing of the issue likely to be successful?
  - Are they playing on more than one chessboard?[5]

The EPA framework is one tool to help time- and resource-constrained development practitioners better apply PEA, especially in the hectic environment of field operations.

Regardless of the PEA approach undertaken by donors, this book underscores the important role that political financing should play in PEA. The flow of money in politics impacts incentives, starting from the problem level. For instance, a donor-funded transport project implemented by a local government may become a source of political funds, which, when extracted, reduce the quality of that project. Soon such behavior might permeate other projects across the transport sector, before ultimately becoming accepted behavior in sectors across the country. The extraction of these funds may finance "free and fair" democratic elections, but in reality, it is stifling development progress. With respect to everyday PEA applied to key decision makers, this book contributes to practitioners' understanding of at least three EPA questions above:

• Do you understand the constraints they face?
• Is it clear who and what the key influences on them are?
• Is their behavior being shaped by social norms about what is appropriate?

The ways in which politicians in developing countries raise funds to conduct election campaigns represent critical constraints that these politicians must face on a daily basis. The providers of those funds can likely gain increased access to these politicians, if not outright influence— influence that can negatively impact the quality of development. And, similar to the American cases of machine politics, these behaviors are likely sealed and sustained by implicit social norms, such as reciprocity.

Political financing is central to how decision makers act and why seemingly beneficial reforms may be stymied. It can be understandably difficult to grasp how political financing works in practice, though. As demonstrated by Baez Camargo and Koechlin (2018), political actors conduct their activities in informal ways, even hiding their illicit actions behind a façade of seemingly legal practices. This book directly investigates political actors' political-financing activities to address a gap in the donor and scholarly PEA literature. Despite pushes for democratization and election transparency in developing countries, there is little theory or evidence of where political candidates and their supporters access funds to conduct campaigns. This book aims to provide such theory and evidence while also advocating for practitioners to think more deeply about how political finance impacts PEA—and subsequently impacts their operations.

The case of Ghana

Political finance by its very nature is secretive and complex; to understand it, we must parachute beneath the treetops of the political ecosystem and explore from the ground level. We must "soak and poke" (Fenno 1990). The landscape of the political ecosystem is shaped by constitutions, formal rules, informal practices, ethnicities, religious beliefs, languages, hierarchies, legal precedents, colonial histories, and many other factors. The inhabitants of this ecosystem include not only politicians, but also the bureaucrats, private businesses, political parties, special interests, traditional authorities, voters, and many others. Strictly quantitative methods such as experiments, regressions, and other statistical techniques are helpful in the study of political ecosystems, but they cannot penetrate the ecosystem's treetops. They cannot earn the trust of a respondent and listen to her confess the truths of how and why the ecosystem works the way it does. Like biological ecosystems, the political ecosystem exhibits periods of overgrowth and undergrowth, equilibria of conflict and cooperation, and fluctuations in the dominance or submission of certain species. But like the biological sphere, inhabitants of the political ecosystem extract underlying resources to survive and thrive. In the political ecosystem, money is the water that flows and permeates throughout. Inhabitants need that water to survive, and they harness it to make their interests flourish. Certain agents of the ecosystem may experience political-finance droughts and temporarily wither, while other agents absorb water and deliver abundant rains elsewhere.

Ghana is a representative African case for many reasons. Attaining independence from the British in 1957, the country experienced coups and military rule, similar to its neighbor, Benin (Riedl 2014). However, since the adoption of a democratic constitution in 1992, Ghana has witnessed peaceful turnovers of power between its two major parties. In the 1990s, many observers viewed Ghana as an African success story, with its sustained levels of private-sector growth and poverty reduction (Armstrong 1996; Killick 2010). Other scholars note problems Ghana shares with peer African countries, namely fiscal deficits and high levels of corruption (van de Walle 1997). Further, Ghana's political parties tend to affiliate with specific ethnic groups, similar to parties in Zambia and Benin (Riedl 2014).

There are numerous entry points into politics for Ghanaians. Administratively, the country consists of 10 regions, which are subdivided into 216 districts. Figure 0.1 presents Ghana's ten regions and their capitals. The lowest political offices in districts are unit committees, which correspond to ward aldermen (Friedrich Ebert Stiftung 2010). Just above the unit committees are District Assembly members, who form the deliberative body at the district level. In each District Assembly, 70% of members are elected by the district's citizens, while the rest are government appointees.[6] The highest office in a district is the District Chief

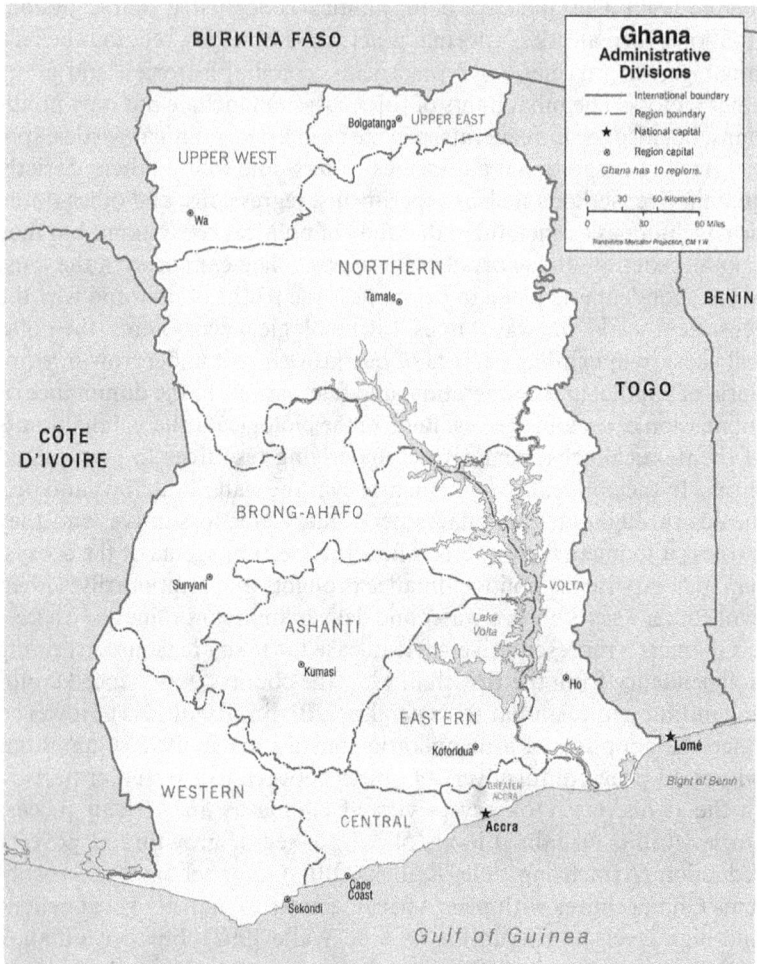

Figure 0.1 Map of Ghana's Ten Regions.
Source: CIA World Factbook, 2007.

Executive (DCE), similar to a mayor. The DCE is appointed by the President and can be removed at any time during the President's term.[7] This person is almost always a member of the President's party. As a result, the governing party holds the highest office in each district, even in areas that are opposition strongholds. The DCE's official task is to ensure that the government's policies are implemented, and she oversees the allocation and monitoring of local projects.

Ghanaian voters elect 275 Members of Parliament (MPs) from single-member constituencies, who serve fixed four-year terms. Most parliamentary constituencies overlap directly with district boundaries, though more populous urban districts have multiple MPs. According to the 1992 Constitution, at least half of the President's Cabinet must be comprised of MPs, which implies that being an MP in the President's party can be a lucrative opportunity. Presidents are elected from a single national constituency and serve fixed four-year terms, coterminous with MPs. Since 1992, Ghana has had five Presidents: all possessed political experience prior to becoming President. Similarly, most Vice Presidents have had political or civil-service experience. In recent years, academics have served as Vice President (John Atta Mills, Kwesi Amissah-Arthur, Mahamudu Bawumia), and these academics all had prior policy experience.

Two parties dominate Ghanaian politics. At the time this book was being researched, the left-leaning National Democratic Congress (NDC) was the ruling party, holding both the presidency and a majority in parliament. The NDC derives its electoral strength from the Volta Region, home of the Ewe ethnic group, as well as the Muslim-majority northern regions. The right-leaning New Patriotic Party (NPP) was the opposition at the time of this study, and they held the presidency and parliament from 2000 to 2008. The NPP's electoral strongholds are the Ashanti and Eastern Regions, which are the homelands of the Akan ethnic groups. It is technically possible for the presidency to be held by one party and parliament by another. Recently, numerous constituencies have voted "skirt-and-blouse", choosing one party's candidate for President and the other party's candidate for MP. Both parties have internal mechanisms for electing party chairs, secretaries, organizers, and other executives at the various levels of organization.

The President of Ghana wields numerous appointment powers. In addition to appointing Cabinet ministers and deputy ministers, the President appoints all 10 Regional Ministers and all 216 DCEs, who are effectively local mayors. However, the President chooses these officials in consultation with the ruling party's executives (at the national and regional levels), and party executives often advance their own candidates. These ministers and DCEs can be replaced at any time, so they are under consistent pressure to satisfy the President's and party's interests.

Methodology

This book's research embeds itself within Ghana's decentralized, district-level bureaucracy—the "front lines" where governing directly impacts and interacts with citizens. While there is a central policy-formulating bureaucracy in Accra, each region and district contains its own policy-implementing bureaucracy. The regions and districts work to implement local club and public goods, such as schools, market stalls, and minor roads. The decentralized bureaucratic apparatus is overseen by the Ministry of Local Government and Rural Development as well as the Local Government Service Secretariat. The District Coordinating Director (DCD) is the bureaucratic head of the district. A veteran member of the public service, she oversees the activities of every bureaucratic sector in the district. The District Finance Officer manages the district's income flows. The District Planning Officer (DPO) assesses the district's development needs. The District Works Engineer oversees procurement and construction. Program areas such as education, health, and agriculture have their own directors. Bureaucrats are appointed via the Local Government Service Secretariat in Accra. Their training is extensive, and many hold graduate degrees in various fields.

I conducted this book's primary fieldwork in Ghana between September 2013 and July 2014. Subsequent fieldwork was conducted in June 2015 so I could interview additional senior-level politicians and party leaders. This project builds off of fieldwork that took place over several trips starting in 2008; in total, more than two years were spent conducting research in Ghana and cultivating relationships with politicians, bureaucrats, and various political players.

I observed 11 districts across all 10 of the country's regions up close, employing multiple research methods. These districts were chosen to ensure regional, ethnic, and political balance in the sample. I lived in each district for up to four weeks, with most days spent embedded at the District Assembly, where I became familiar to the political leadership, bureaucrats, and other notables. For the highest-level politicians and officers, I conducted in-depth, semi-structured interviews, devoting one to three hours per interview. My residence in each district allowed for numerous informal discussions, whether at residences, at drinking spots, or in vehicles. I participated in assembly meetings and project inspections. Beyond politicians and bureaucrats, numerous interviews and focus groups were conducted with former DCEs, party officials, construction contractors, and traditional chiefs. Retired politicians and party chairs were especially valuable confidants, as they had less to lose from speaking openly. A note on methods: I am frequently asked, "How did you get people to talk about such sensitive issues?" This project was enhanced by living in each district and spending significant amounts of time interacting with people. Familiarity turned to trust, and many interviewees welcomed the cathartic chance to tell their stories and open up without judgment. Overall, I interviewed nearly 200 individuals.

To understand the roots of political finance, it is necessary to conduct research at the local levels. Though a small country, Ghana encompasses a variety of political, ethnic, and historical cleavages. Simply staying close to Accra or another large city might bias results, especially if rural districts experience very different political dynamics and demands. At the district level, one may observe a variety of close interactions between politicians—especially DCEs and MPs—as well as within and between the two major political parties. It is possible that these actions are typically cordial, but they may also be acrimonious. Within the set of DCEs there may be variation, with some DCEs content to stay in their current office and serve one term, while other DCEs are keen to run for higher offices. Eleven districts were ultimately selected for this study. One district (District A) served as a pilot to test questions for the elite interviews and bureaucrat surveys, while ten districts were selected for the main part of this research. Each of the ten regions had one district in the main study. Bureaucrats in each of the ten main districts received the same interview questions concerning their background, job duties, role in procurement, political affiliations, and so forth. For all of these districts, the overarching research goal was to examine how "cleanly" each district was managing its development resources and to get to the bottom of how Ghana's politics is financed.

Sampling of districts took several criteria into account. Each district has a DCE selected by the ruling party (NDC, at the time of this study), but MPs come from either the NDC or the NPP in my sample. I ensured that there was balance between districts where both major politicians were from the NDC and districts where the DCE was from the NDC, and the MP was from the NPP. Districts where DCEs and MPs are from the same party might be managed more cleanly relative to districts where the DCEs and MPs are from different parties. One could hypothesize that districts where the DCE and the MP were of different parties might witness contentious relations as the two jockey to "credit claim" development projects (Mayhew 1974); however, that was not always the case. Conversely, I often—but not always—witnessed acrimonious relations between DCEs and MPs of the same party, as these individuals typically contested against each other in parliamentary primaries.

As evidenced by their sometimes hostile relations with MPs, DCEs differ in their types of political ambition (Schlesinger 1966). Many DCEs aspire to be MPs since that office is seen as more secure—DCEs can be removed from office at any time, while MPs are fairly secure in their four-year terms. It is possible that there are differences in how cleanly a district is run for districts that have DCEs with Parliamentary ambitions as opposed to districts whose DCEs do not have Parliamentary ambitions. I included some districts where the DCE had campaigned for Parliament in the prior election in 2012 and districts where the DCE had not campaigned in 2012.

In Ghana, DCEs serve at the pleasure of the President, and they can be reappointed to additional terms once their original mandate expires. It is possible that DCEs who have been appointed to their second or third terms are more experienced and will run their districts more cleanly than DCEs who are new and in their first terms. In my sample, I selected districts in which the DCE had been previously appointed and districts where the DCE was newly appointed.

In terms of overall sample composition, I provided that at least one of the districts was newly created. At each census, the Government of Ghana can create additional districts to account for population growth and ensure that its citizens can continue to access local-government services. I also selected three urban districts, which are known as "municipal" and "metropolitan" assemblies, corresponding to the rural-urban composition of Ghana's (at the time) 216 districts. Of the 11 districts in my sample, 7 had DCEs that ran for Parliament in 2012, while 4 had DCEs that did not run for Parliament. Six districts had DCEs and MPs from different parties, while five districts had DCEs and MPs who were both from the NDC. Similarly, six districts had first-term DCEs, while five districts had DCEs with prior experience. Short descriptions of each district follow below. Throughout this book, I will refer to respondents by their district's letter, where applicable. Occasionally, to further protect the confidentiality of particular respondents, I may also refer to the ecological zone of their district: districts belonging to the Northern, Upper East, and Upper West Regions lie in the savannah zone; districts belonging to the Ashanti, Brong Ahafo, and Eastern Regions lie in the transitional zone; and districts belonging to the Central, Greater Accra, Volta, and Western Regions lie in the coastal zone.

District A, Brong Ahafo Region (pilot district)

This district lies in the Brong Ahafo Region. District A is located in the forested to transitional climate zone of the country. Similar to neighboring areas, this district's economy is primarily based in agriculture and livestock-raising, and the district possesses ample forest resources which fuel the timber trade. The district also sees significant gold-mining action from various international companies. This pilot district was chosen from the Brong Ahafo Region because that region has been a "swing" area in prior Presidential elections and also lies between the coastal and northern zones of the country.

District B, Upper East Region

This district lies in the Upper East Region, near the border with Burkina Faso. This district is known for its rolling hills and traditional religious shrines. As this district lies in the North, it is hot year-round with wet and dry seasons. During the dry season from October through April, daytime temperatures can exceed 110F. The district's primary economic activity is agriculture, employing 75% of the population. The main vegetation of this district is Guinea savannah woodland, with economically important trees including baobab, shea nut, dawadawa, and acacia.

District C, Upper West Region

This district is in the Upper West Region and is generally flat and low-lying. Similar to District B, this district is hot and dry, with a pronounced harmattan season (dry season prone to dusty conditions). Agriculture is the major source of employment in District C, with baobab, shea nuts, dawadawa, and acacia again being the main tree crops. This district's Guinea savannah grasses are also suitable for raising livestock, particularly cattle, sheep, goats, pigs, and poultry.

District D, Northern Region

District D is an urban district of the Northern Region of Ghana, featuring a mix of Guinea savannah woodland and is part of the Volta River basin. This district is generally flat, but parts of it are quite hilly. Similar to districts in Upper East and Upper West, this district experiences a hot and dry climate, with harmattan winds blowing dust from the Sahara. Agriculture is a main source of employment, with major crops including rice, groundnuts, yams, cassava, and sorghum.

District E, Brong Ahafo Region

District E is in the Brong Ahafo Region, close to Cote d'Ivoire. Agricultural smuggling (particularly of cocoa) is a problem in this district.

The district's topography is undulating, with elevations ranging from 150 to 600 meters above sea level. District E lies within the wet semi-equatorial zone, and its main vegetation consists of woodland timber, with odum, mahogany, and teak being harvested in the district. Food and cash crop production remains the main economic activity of the district—cashews, yams, maize, and tomatoes are prevalent.

District F, Ashanti Region

District F is located in the Ashanti Region and is close to the border with the Brong Ahafo Region. This district contains many hills and numerous rivers. Over 80% of this district's population is engaged in farming. The district's climate favors the production of cocoa, citrus, palm oil, maize, rice, and various other crops. In District F, the major ethnic group is the Akan, who follow different land-ownership and inheritance structures compared to ethnic groups in the more northern districts.

District G, Eastern Region

District G is located in the Eastern Region, close to the border of Ashanti Region. Geographically, this district features undulating topography and experiences two rainy seasons each year. District G is located at a higher elevation in the wet, forested region of Ghana, though it also contains savannah. Much of this district's population works in agriculture, with key crops including cocoa, maize, cassava, yams, and groundnuts.

District H, Volta Region

District H is a new district of Volta Region, having been created in 2012. This area, like much of the Volta Region, is populated by the Ewe ethnic group, though the Guan ethnic group forms a substantial minority. This district is forested and hilly, with most of the population engaged in agriculture.

District J, Greater Accra Region[8]

District J is located in the Greater Accra Region. Geographically, this district features coastal savannah and is generally flat, though parts of the district are hilly. Many residents of this district are engaged in livestock production and fishing. From a climate perspective, District

J features two rainy seasons each year, and its land is suitable for growing maize, cassava, rice, tomatoes, and export-quality vegetables. Despite this district's proximity to the national capital, Accra, it has rural areas and various infrastructural deficiencies.

District K, Central Region

District K, in the Central Region, is an urban district. Forestry is an important economic activity in this district, and much of the district is characterized by valleys and steep hills. Similar to other southern districts, District K experiences two rainy seasons each year. Beyond forestry, approximately half of the land in this district is devoted to cocoa production; other important crops include maize, plantain, cassava, and cocoyam. Gold mining is another economically significant activity in District K, but the district must contend with illegal miners, known as *galamsey*, whose methods pollute the local environment.

District L, Western Region

District L, located in the Western Region, is the third urban district of my sample. Like many of the southern districts, District L features two rainy seasons each year. Agriculture employs approximately 25% of the people in District L, but a majority of residents work in services and small-scale business. Other notable economic activities include fishing, gari production, and groundnut processing.

I also reviewed public-goods and contract data from each district. While each district is nominally supposed to report projects and contracts to the Ministry of Local Government and Rural Development, in practice, this does not regularly happen. Such data is rarely publicly available. However, most districts did provide their 2012 Annual Action Plans, which include basic data on contracts. The quality of the data differs significantly between districts. While in Accra, I obtained additional data on construction contractors and qualifications from the then-Ministry of Water Resources, Works, and Housing.

Plan of the book

Chapter 1 introduces four model individuals representing politicians, bureaucrats, construction contractors, and political-party chairs. Chapter 2 describes a district's sealed-bid procurement meeting witnessed by the author that illuminated political-finance dynamics in Ghana. This chapter then draws from the author's fieldwork across

Ghana to develop a model of how political financing actually operates. Chapter 3 addresses the question of how this political-financing model sustains itself across party changes in government through the risk aversion of contractors and social norms of reciprocity. The Conclusion connects this volume's theory of political financing with Ostrom's (1990) work on managing common-pool resources to provide a novel way forward to improve club- and public-goods delivery—a way forward that overturns a key institutional requirement of most development practitioners. I then generalize this recommendation to an approach that donors can use to incorporate political-finance considerations in their work and offer ideas for future areas of research.

This book is intended for scholars, practitioners, and students engaged in the political economy of international development. Political finance is a little explored frontier of the social sciences, particularly in the context of developing countries, but it is at the heart of incentives, actions, and outcomes. A country's economic and social development cannot be separated from the practices that govern how its decision makers earn and maintain power. If decision makers owe some entity for their office, that entity may exercise influence over that decision maker. While the political ecosystem often shows cooperation and symbiosis, it can also be ruthless to individuals who attempt to circumvent its formal and informal rules. Many of these individuals have the intrinsic desire to serve the public, but unfortunately they are compromised by the need to generate money for political activities. Political financing should be integrated into each donor's PEA strategy and anti-corruption programing. It can be easy for donors to decry seemingly corrupt behaviors, but donors must fully understand why such behaviors occur and then reflect on whether they would act any differently if they found themselves in that ecosystem.

Notes

1 While there are many other political actors, depending on the country context, this book will primarily focus on politicians, bureaucrats, construction contractors, and party leadership.
2 In the development context, politicians' motive to credit claim is an opportunity for donors to secure political support by designating some projects as quick, visible wins.
3 However, it is not necessarily the case that party leaders only support their party's loyalists. Sometimes they help those who support opposition parties, whether out of kinship obligations, expectations of future assistance, or personal relationships.
4 See also the Thinking and Working Politically Working Group, https://twpcommunity.org.

5 Please refer to Hudson, Marquette, and Waldock (2016) for additional material and follow-up questions to each of these questions.
6 These government appointees help the national government to ensure that a particular District Assembly has a majority loyal to the party in power.
7 However, as this book is going to press, Ghana plans to hold a referendum in late 2019 to determine whether DCEs should be locally elected.
8 To avoid confusion with numbers, the letter I was skipped in my classification of sampled districts.

References

Acemoglu, Daron, Simon Johnson, and James Robinson 2001. "The Colonial Origins of Comparative Development: An Empirical Investigation." *American Economic Review*, 91(5): 1369–1401.

Achebe, Chinua. 1960. *No Longer at Ease*. London: Heinemann.

Alesina, Alberto and Guido Tabellini. 2007. "Bureaucrats or Politicians? Part I: A Single Policy Task." *American Economic Review*, 97: 169–179.

Armstrong, Robert. 1996. "Ghana Country Assistance Review: A Study in Development Effectiveness." World Bank Operations Evaluation Study, Report No. 15349.

Baez Camargo, Claudia and Lucy Koechlin. 2018. "Informal Governance: Comparative Perspectives on Co-optation, Control, and Camouflage in Rwanda, Tanzania and Uganda." *International Development Policy*, 10: 78–100.

Blundo, Giorgio and Jean-Pierre Olivier de Sardan. 2006. *Everyday Corruption and the State*. London: Zed Books.

Brierley, Sarah. 2019a. "Unprincipled Principals: Co-Opted Bureaucrats and Corruption in Ghana." *American Journal of Political Science*. Forthcoming.

Brierley, Sarah. 2019b. "Combining Patronage and Merit in Public-Sector Recruitment." *Journal of Politics*, Forthcoming.

Carothers, Thomas and Diane de Gramont. 2013. *Development Aid Confronts Politics: The Almost Revolution*. Washington, DC: Carnegie Endowment for International Peace.

Carpenter, Daniel. 2001. *The Forging of Bureaucratic Autonomy: Reputations, Networks, and Policy Innovation in Executive Agencies, 1862–1928*. Princeton, NJ: Princeton University Press.

Department for International Development (DFID). 2009. "Political Economy Analysis How to Note." URL: https://www.odi.org/sites/odi.org.uk/files/odi-assets/events-documents/3797.pdf

Downs, Anthony. 1967. *Inside Bureaucracy*. Boston, MA: Little, Brown.

Ekeh, Peter. 1975. "Colonialism and the Two Publics in Africa: A Theoretical Statement." *Comparative Studies in Society and History*, 17(1): 91–112.

Fenno, Richard. 1978. *Home Style: House Members in Their Districts*. Boston, MA: Little, Brown.

Fenno, Richard. 1990. *Watching Politicians: Essays on Participant Observation*. Berkeley, CA: Institute of Governmental Studies Press.

Friedrich Ebert Stiftung. 2010. "A Guide to District Assemblies in Ghana." URL: http://library.fes.de/pdf-files/bueros/ghana/10487-entsichert-a%20guide%20 to%20district%20assemblies%20pressbk_decrypt.pdf

Gingerich, Daniel. 2013. *Political Institutions and Party-Directed Corruption in South America: Stealing for the Team.* Cambridge, UK: Cambridge University Press.

Hanna, Rema and Shing-Yi Wang. 2017. "Dishonesty and Selection into Public Service: Evidence from India." *American Economic Journal: Economic Policy*, American Economic Association, 9(3): 262–290.

Hudson, David, Heather Marquette, and Sam Waldock. 2016. "Everyday Political Economy Analysis." URL: https://www.dlprog.org/publications/ research-papers/everyday-political-analysis

Ichino, Nahomi and Noah Nathan. 2013. "Crossing the Line: Local Ethnic Geography and Voting in Ghana." *American Political Science Review*, 107(2): 344–361.

Jakupec, Viktor and Max Kelly. 2019. *Foreign Aid in the Age of Populism: Political Economy Analysis from Washington to Beijing.* Abingdon, UK: Routledge.

Johnson, Chalmers. 1982. *MITI and the Japanese Miracle: The Growth of Industrial Policy: 1925–1975.* Stanford, CA: Stanford University Press.

Kalla, Joshua and David Broockman. 2015. "Campaign Contributions Facilitate Access to Congressional Officials: A Randomized Field Experiment." *American Journal of Political Science,* 60(3): 545–558.

Kaufman, Herbert. 1960. *The Forest Ranger: A Study in Administrative Behavior.* Washington, DC: Resources for the Future.

Killick, Tony. 2010. *Development Economics in Action: A Study of Economic Policies in Ghana.* New York, NY: Routledge.

Leftwich, Adrian. 2007. "From Drivers of Change to the Politics of Development: Refining the Analytical Framework to Understand the Politics of the Places Where We Work." URL: http://www.gsdrc.org/docs/open/doc105.pdf

Lessig, Lawrence. 2011. *Republic, Lost: How Money Corrupts Congress—And a Plan to Stop It.* New York, NY: Twelve.

Lindberg, Staffan. 2010. "What Accountability Pressures Do MPs in Africa Face and How Do They Respond? Evidence from Ghana." *Journal of Modern African Studies*, 48(1): 117–142.

Lipsky, Michael. 1980. *Street-Level Bureaucracy: Dilemmas of the Individual in Public Service.* New York, NY: Russell Sage Foundation.

Mayhew, David. 1974. *Congress: The Electoral Connection.* New Haven, CT: Yale University Press.

Norris, Pippa and Andrea Abel van Es, eds. 2016. *Checkbook Elections? Political Finance in Comparative Perspective.* Oxford, UK: Oxford University Press.

Ostrom, Elinor. 1990. *Governing the Commons: The Evolution of Institutions for Collective Action.* Cambridge, UK: Cambridge University Press.

Posner, Daniel. 2005. *Institutions and Ethnic Politics in Africa.* Cambridge, UK: Cambridge University Press.

Powell, Lynda. 2014. "The Influence of Campaign Contributions on the Legislative Process." *Duke Journal of Constitutional Law and Public Policy*, 9(1): 75–101.

Power, Sam. 2016. "The British Party Funding Regime at a Critical Juncture? Applying New Institutional Analysis." *Politics*, 37(2): 134–150.

Power, Sam. 2018. "Party Funding Regimes and Corruption in Western Europe: A Comparative Study of Great Britain and Denmark." PhD Thesis, University of Sussex.

Price, Robert. 1975. *Society and Bureaucracy in Contemporary Ghana*. Berkeley: University of California Press.

Rasul, Imran and Daniel Rogger. 2018. "Management of Bureaucrats and Public Service Delivery: Evidence from the Nigerian Civil Service." *Economic Journal*, 128(608): 413–446.

Rasul, Imran, Daniel Rogger, and Martin Williams. 2018. "Management and Bureaucratic Effectiveness: Evidence from the Ghanaian Civil Service." World Bank Policy Research Working Paper, No. 8595.

Riedl, Rachel Beatty. 2014. *Authoritarian Origins of Democratic Party Systems in Africa*. New York, NY: Cambridge University Press.

Riordon, William. 1905. *Plunkitt of Tammany Hall: A Series of Very Plain Talks on Very Practical Politics*. New York, NY: McClure, Phillips & Co.

Royko, Mike. 1971. *Boss: Richard J. Daley of Chicago*. Boston, MA: E.P. Dutton.

Schlesinger, Joseph. 1966. *Ambition and Politics: Political Careers in the United States*. Chicago, IL: Rand McNally.

Schneer, Benjamin and Maxwell Palmer. 2016. "Capitol Gains: The Returns to Elected Office from Corporate Board Directorships." *Journal of Politics*, 78(1): 181–196.

Sigman, Rachel. 2015. "Which Jobs for Which Boys? Party Financing, Patronage, and State Capacity in African Democracies." PhD Dissertation, Syracuse University.

Skowronek, Stephen. 1982. *Building a New American State*. Cambridge, UK: Cambridge University Press.

Toeba, Thato. 2018. "Corruption in Public Procurement in Lesotho." *The Law and Development Review*, 11(2): 397–431.

van de Walle, Nicolas. 1997. *African Economies and the Politics of Permanent Crisis, 1979–1999*. New York, NY: Cambridge University Press.

van de Walle, Nicolas. 2007. "Meet the New Boss, Same as the Old Boss? The Evolution of Political Clientelism in Africa." In Herbert Kitschelt and Steve Wilkinson (eds.) *Patrons or Policies? Patterns of Democratic Accountability and Political Competition*, 50–67. New York, NY: Cambridge University Press.

Weber, Max. 1922 [1978]. *Economy and Society*. Berkeley: University of California Press.

Wilson, James. 1989. *Bureaucracy*. New York, NY: Basic Books.

Woodall, Brian. 1996. *Japan under Construction: Corruption, Politics, and Public Works*. Berkeley: University of California Press.

1 Politicians, bureaucrats, contractors, and chairs

Political ecosystems are complex and interdependent. There can be many players in that ecosystem, including politicians, bureaucrats, traditional leaders, civil society, the private sector, and so forth. In a given society, many forces cut across the ecosystem, shaping dependencies and behavioral patterns. Though "modern" democratic constitutions shape the electoral practices of many countries, there are still underlying forces that shape political actions and outcomes—ethnicity, religion, history, colonialism, to name a few. This book argues that such histories and practices can even stabilize underlying corrupt behavior, despite visible changes in political leadership. To understand such an ecosystem, it is crucial to examine a case deeply.

Political ambitions, bureaucrats' social obligations, and party organizations must all be financed. I posit that each of the players discussed in this chapter is essential to the functioning of Ghanaian politics. Development outcomes are suboptimal, and to understand Ghana's challenges in providing quality public goods, one must understand political financing. I describe below a representative District Chief Executive (DCE), senior bureaucrat, construction contractor, and regional party chair. All names have been changed to protect respondents' privacy. In addition, I supplement the DCE, bureaucrat, and contractor descriptions with quantitative data drawn from archives as well as surveys and interviews that I administered to a broader sample of DCEs, bureaucrats, and contractors.

The players

The politician

Appointed in 2012, Olivia Amadu is DCE of a district in the coastal zone of the country, well populated and located around Ghana's forest belt. Agriculture and forestry are this district's main sources of income, and its topography is varied, with numerous rivers, valleys, and rocky hills. Approximately half of the land in the district is dedicated to cocoa, Ghana's major export crop. Plantains, cassava, cocoyam, livestock, and fish-farming are other important agricultural sectors. Like many of its surrounding districts, Amadu's district has problems with illegal—or *galamsey*—miners who mine gold and other valuable resources, inflicting serious harm to the district's ecology. Similar to its surrounding districts, Amadu's district is predominantly Akan in ethnicity, and the most widely practiced religion is Pentecostalism.

Amadu's district favors the NPP (New Patriotic Party, the national opposition), though it is more politically competitive than surrounding districts. An NDC member, Amadu contested the NDC parliamentary primary against the local party chairman in 2012, but did not win; instead, she was appointed DCE after the general election. A native of this area, Amadu explains that her family has always been involved in politics. Family political involvement is a common theme for DCEs; typically, a father or an uncle had been involved with a political organization many years before. For Amadu, two brothers have been involved in politics, with one holding political office and the other being a leader within the NDC. In addition to political office, family members of Amadu have been traditional chiefs and queen mothers. She greatly admired her brothers, and her family is drawn to the social-democratic nature of the NDC, a party that she claims treats all people as equals. For Amadu, her experiences as a woman further motivated her decision to enter politics; after seeing the women of her mother's village suffer, Amadu decided to help them. Initially, she lobbied NGOs to assist these women, but later decided a political career would be more effective. Amadu is well educated. Still young, she attained her first degree from a prominent Ghanaian university in the early 2000s. Amadu later received her executive MBA. In her relatively short professional life, she has held several private and public positions.

Amadu harbors progressive (in Schlesinger's 1966 formulation) political ambitions, and many of the DCEs in my sample share this stance. Talking about elections, I find her overly boastful, implying a security of position that is actually lacking. She is a stalwart NDC politician, and is highly critical of the opposition NPP, which is not a common sentiment amongst other DCEs in my sample, most of whom respect the opposition party. She is not willing to cooperate with the NPP. For her, it is clear that the NDC is the party of the people,

> My party, we don't talk much. We help people, ensure roads are good. We are the party for women and children—we don't go on

air just to talk. [...] At election time, people vote on performance, and others will be disappointed.

Of the DCEs in my sample, Amadu is one of several who can talk of actual physical accomplishments in their districts rather than just big ideas. Throughout our interview, she emphasizes her accomplishments in great detail, as if ready to campaign at a moment's notice.

> Since I have come, we have built 25 boreholes. And I have been here less than one year!

In terms of campaigning, she is confident of the NDC's fortunes in this district,

> In 2008, our candidate for Parliament had only 5,000 votes, but the NPP candidate won with 17,000. In 2012, the NPP had 15,000, while the NDC had 13,000. In 2016, we will take the seat.

Despite losing the 2012 parliamentary primary to a party chairman, Amadu remained confident in her abilities and the NDC's fortunes. Similar to many Ghanaian citizens, she places great faith in God's plan,

> You know, I contested at that time against [a then-executive of the party]. We went around, and I visited all the villages twice before I had a medical issue. I believe in God, and I am not surprised that I lost. I did all possible to win. My contender knew I was going to win.
>
> With the chairman, I came here, this young lady with an attractive CV. People saw me as a threat. Some people were calling others, namely the men, not to vote for me. The way this lady (me) is, she may go far.

Even though she campaigned against a party executive, Amadu was still selected as DCE. As Schlesinger (1966) notes, politicians' incentives can be framed by the higher offices available to them. For a DCE, the next higher office is that of Member of Parliament (MP). Being an MP confers numerous advantages over being a DCE. A DCE can be removed from office at any time by the President, and this removal is especially likely if the DCE loses favor with her local party executives. An MP, on the other hand, serves a fixed four-year term. If a politician is motivated by profit, then being elected as MP would allow them to network with large corporations and donors in Accra. According to my calculations, in the 2012 parliamentary election, 52 sitting DCEs (of then-170 total) contested for parliament, at either the primary- or general-election stage. Thirteen DCEs ultimately prevailed. The attractiveness of parliamentary office can poison relations between a district's DCE and its MP(s), regardless of their party affiliations. Amadu faces a hostile party executive board in the district, which, as many DCEs reported to me, could make one's life difficult with demands for money; there are various coping strategies DCEs take to mitigate those challenges. Amadu's tense relationship with party executives mirrors the experiences described by many other DCEs I interviewed. Party executives can hamper a DCE's agenda through their influence on the procurement process or by cultivating opposition. Party executives can also try to bend a DCE's agenda to their will. For this DCE, she avoids some of these challenges by turning to the outside to ensure that her district's development needs are well served,

> I have been lobbying [international organizations] since I came here. I go out, and I market my district! I got two six-room classroom blocks! I lobby.

Lobby is a favorite euphemism of this DCE. When I ask DCEs about pressures they face when awarding contracts, most concede significant pressure and moral dilemma. Most DCEs highlight the need to get contractors to perform well, but I found no DCEs who were able to ensure quality work. While Amadu acknowledges such challenges, she embraces the pressure that party contractors place on her,

> Pressure from contractors? Oh, that is called lobbying! I condemn contractors who can't perform. If we know people who perform, we can give it to them. But it is hard to know who can perform.

Other DCEs find pressure from contractors and community members more frustrating, however,

> When there are demands from communities, you have to explain it. There is a process—don't just have money in my purse. There is a procurement law—but people don't want to hear it. Let people understand the limits of your power.
>
> DCE, District G

> It is about the MONEY! The people keep coming to you. 'I am bereaved, I have to pay school fees, my wife is admitted (to hospital).' And so forth. They expect money from you. It is especially

bad with party people! They think that because you are DCE that you can just open up the district budget to them. But that is not the case!

DCE, District F

Regarding her relationship with bureaucrats, Amadu is a commander. She emphasizes her superiority over the bureaucrats and that she wants to implement policies quickly.

I always tell them, 'I am a politician with short time.' They are re-laxed. At times, I push them. We don't have time; we must perform now. If we want to go to tender, you must prepare the documents.

Many bureaucrats across my sample reported being rushed by their DCEs to prepare tendering documents. DCEs, in turn, face pressure from constituents regarding the award of contracts.

Amadu is a young politician with progressive ambitions for higher office (Schlesinger 1966). She is energetic, with a willingness to cater to party contractors and gain exposure. Her time as DCE builds both her credentials and her funding base. She hails from a competitive area, one that the NDC desires to ensure national victory. Further, attitudes towards women in Ghanaian politics, at least at the highest levels, are changing, meaning that she could be well placed to reach the top. When I asked Amadu where she envisioned herself in five years' time she confidently assured me,

Oh, my party will still be in power. And I will be a deputy minis-ter, at least.

The most difficult challenge Amadu faces is governing with a hostile party-executive board in her district. While it is possible that she can obtain higher office without their support, she would be more likely to win primaries with their favor. Many DCEs in Ghana have been ousted from their position by jealous party executives, so Amadu must find a way to satisfy their needs.

The bureaucrat

Yusuf Massoud is the District Coordinating Director (DCD) of a ru-ral district located near a city in the coastal zone of Ghana. Despite its proximity to a city, this district lacks many modern amenities that were found in rural districts further north. Massoud's district features coastal savannah and is flat in topography. Economically, this district is involved in livestock production, but also grows traditional crops.

Politically, Massoud's district is located in a very competitive region, similar to DCE Amadu's district, though in previous elections, it has tended to support the NDC for both president and parliament. Like several other districts, Massoud's was subdivided within the past five years, with a portion becoming an entirely new district. With each census, new districts are created to ensure population balance.

My first full day in the district, I met the DCE. Unlike the other DCEs in my sample, this one was not initially welcoming towards me. He did not understand why I would need to visit a district in every region of the country,

> Oh, it is the same everywhere! You have the same structures and policies!

To him, I was wasting my time. The DCD, Massoud, however, was very different in attitude from the DCE. Entering Massoud's office, just across the hall, the environment was relaxed, and I greeted several senior bureaucrats while chatting with him. I explained that I wished to study the relationship between politicians and bureaucrats in Ghana's local government.

> That is a very thorny issue you raise there. It depends very much on the personality of the politician in charge. Anyways, you will need some candid responses.

As each senior bureaucrat heard my topic, they chuckled in a knowing fashion. Compared to other districts in my sample, the bureaucrats of this district were the most unified in their assessment of political ambitions and its negative effect on bureaucratic decision-making. While Massoud is my focus, I will include the perspectives of other bureaucrats in this section.

Massoud is a native of a northern region of Ghana and is well educated, holding an MBA. Like many DCDs, he has completed coursework at the prestigious Ghana Institute of Management and Public Administration. He has been a member of the public service for over 20 years. Joining the public service so that he could "contribute to the development of rural areas", he has worked in numerous districts and several regions. This notion of contributing to development is a common theme amongst DCDs and other bureaucrats, and the civil service is a respected profession in Ghana.[1] In my sample, most DCDs will stay in one region, but work in several districts of that region; while Massoud has primarily worked within one region, he also has experience outside it. As to why he had served in so many districts, some for very short periods of time,

> That's a part of the system. Whenever there is a change in government, the DCD is moved around. This causes friction.

Many other Ghanaians serving as local-government bureaucrats have had similar experiences to Massoud. To sharpen my insights into the challenges faced by Ghana's local-government bureaucrats, I interviewed 83 other senior bureaucrats across all 10 regions of Ghana. These bureaucrats held such positions as district engineer, finance officer, planner, and so forth. The bureaucrats in my sample worked in both urban and rural districts. Each interview lasted from one to almost four hours.

Table 1.1 presents demographics and levels of experience of the 83 bureaucrats that I interviewed and who collectively provided insights to this study. On average, these senior bureaucrats were, at the time of this study, in their mid-40s. Since Ghana's retirement age for civil servants is set at 60, these bureaucrats hold their senior positions for approximately 15–20 years. On average, senior bureaucrats have 16 years of experience in the civil service. They have typically worked in their district (at the time of interview) for 4.5 years, ranging from

Table 1.1 Demographics and Experience Levels of Bureaucrat Sample

Region	Number of Interviewees	Serving in Home Region (%)	Age	Experience	Years in District
All	83	47.0	44.2	16	4.5
Ashanti	7	85.7	42	12.5	2.4
Brong Ahafo	10	30.0	46	20.3	6.7
Central	7	28.6	42.9	11.9	3.1
Eastern	8	37.5	40.8	12.5	6.5
G. Accra	7	14.3	45	15.6	5.3
Northern	9	66.7	44.4	17.4	3.7
Upper East	10	50.0	45.0	19.3	6.9
Upper West	10	50.0	44.2	14.3	1.4
Volta	8	62.5	43.1	14.5	1.6
Western	7	28.6	47.7	18.3	7.6

Source: Author's data collection and analysis.

1.4 years in Upper West Region to 6.9 years in Upper East Region. On average, almost half of the bureaucrats in my sample are working in the regions in which they were born.

On average, bureaucrats in Ghana earn decent salaries and are well educated. As shown in Table 1.2, on average, approximately 87% of local-government senior bureaucrats have earned *at least* a Bachelor's degree. To supplement their expertise, bureaucrats reported attending, on average, six capacity-building workshops each year. Bureaucrats in the Northern Region attended such workshops most frequently, perhaps because many NGOs maintain offices in Tamale, the Northern Region's capital. In terms of income, local-government senior bureaucrats earn almost 15,000 Ghana cedis a year in base salary, which at the time of study amounted to $6,000 per year, well above Ghana's average per capita income. Nonetheless, these bureaucrats sought more income. Approximately 45% of bureaucrats in my sample reported having secondary sources of income, while also earning, on average, an additional 1,739 cedis per year in per diem pay related to attending workshops. Bureaucrats in the Greater Accra and Western Regions, who are close to major urban areas, earned the highest average per diem pay in my sample.

Across Ghana's ten regions, there are similarities amongst senior bureaucrats' age, income, level of education, and various other factors. Unfortunately, of these senior bureaucrats, there are many similar stories of difficulties in working with politicians. Depending on a bureaucrat's regional or ethnic background or their work with a prior

Table 1.2 Educational Background and Remuneration of Bureaucrat Sample

Region	Tertiary Education (%)	Workshops	Salary	Other Jobs (%)	Per Diem
All	87.0	6	14,508	45.1	1,739
Ashanti	100.0	6.14	13,650	50.0	1,463
Brong Ahafo	90.0	6.5	14,459	60.0	1,157
Central	86.0	5.5	12,943	71.4	1,460
Eastern	87.5	3.06	10,808	0.0	836
Greater Accra	100.0	7.29	14,539	71.4	2,198
Northern	100.0	8.61	13,650	33.3	763
Upper East	70.0	6	13,389	70.0	1,005
Upper West	80.0	7.45	13,696	20.0	1,005
Volta	75.0	3.19	15,207	37.5	1,073
Western	86.0	7.57	23,033	42.9	3,388

Source: Author's data collection and analysis.

administration, a politician may view bureaucrats as partisan and not "on their side". As Massoud recounts,

> In terms of engaging with the DCE, we are supposed to work in harmony. But there are individual differences. Politicians are sometimes not administrators, and sometimes they pigeonhole you—they may perceive you as for or against them. [...] They will look at your background. I'm from one of the northern regions; I will be perceived as NDC. If I am from Ashanti Region, I will be perceived as NPP. If from Volta, they will think I am an NDC man. They will also look at your experience. For instance, in one district I was in, I worked well with the DCE at the time, who was NPP. In 2008, there was a change in government, and an NDC DCE came in. The agitations were very high, and it was perceived that I was with the NPP—even though I am a northerner in background! I am supposed to serve the government of the day.

Massoud also highlights that a politician's level of education and his appreciation for democratic government can impact the relationship between that politician and a bureaucrat,

> The relationship will work well if the politician has an appreciable level of formal education. [...] You may work with a politician who doesn't understand vision of government so he introduces personal issues into administration of the district.

While there are many stories across my sample of politicians introducing "personal issues" into government and questioning the loyalty of their bureaucrats, it is not always the case that bureaucrats are innocent of using their office for personal gain. Massoud asserts that many public servants have taken advantage of the system to extract resources, particularly if politicians are unaware or inexperienced,

> DCDs sometimes go wrongly to exploit ignorance of DCE. I would not say that public servants are not corrupt.

For Massoud, extended families and social expectations exert pressure. As noted above, bureaucrats often serve in their home regions. Such proximity to extended family and friends can amplify pressure on bureaucrats to misuse their office to deliver funds and private goods. Nonetheless, with the wide distribution of mobile phones and banking, even bureaucrats serving far away from their home regions likely feel pressure from extended family and friends.

Outside of financial pressures from family and friends, many bureaucrats, including Massoud, affirmed that saving for retirement was a chief concern. Bureaucrats complained of low salaries and strong social pressure to build a nice house prior to mandatory retirement at age 60. If a bureaucrat fails to complete his house by 60, he may face social ridicule and its associated stress. As demonstrated above, approximately half of the senior bureaucrats in my sample reported benefiting from another source of income. Such sources of income reported to me include operating a farm, driving a taxi, managing private stores—as well as potential conflicts of interests such as offering consulting services and owning a construction firm. These additional sources of income can facilitate a bureaucrat's retirement savings, but they can also be an incentive towards corruption. As noted by other bureaucrats I interviewed,

> That very last question (on preparation for retirement) is the bean of corruption. [...] I am always looking for outside work to supplement my salary.
>
> District Planning Officer, District B

> First and foremost, in Ghana, we think of housing and start preparing for that. Civil servants—using money to build a house and we get loans from bank. Stress will be on you if you build after you retire. [...] Foremost is to get a house. Second is to educate your children. For me, when I started work, my children were small and you just buy small to build your house. Stay focused on plan.
>
> District Agricultural Officer, District C

Though Massoud faces numerous social and retirement pressures, he has made investments that "cushion" him, and he has his businesses on the side. Many public servants report owning their own businesses, but, given their low salaries, it is not clear how they raise the initial capital to start a business.

Local-government bureaucrats in Ghana, like in many other countries, participate in reviewing and awarding contracts to provide public goods and services. However, while Ghana does have formal legislation to safeguard the procurement process, in practice public procurement is a tempting means to reward supporters and extract funds for private use. On the contract-awarding process, Massoud explains the challenges bureaucrats face and how they cope with political demands,

> In all my years in the public service, I have never seen a contract awarded on merit.
> Politicians have friction because they know they have a maximum term, but a public servant has until the age of 60. Politician thinks that when he comes he wants to make the best of his years. This leads to corrupt practices. Some lack an understanding of the rules and regulations—they want public servant to set aside rules, regulations, and laws to do what is expedient. We have a procurement law (Act 663). Politicians would want you to initiate a development project without going through process. You must use diplomacy: let him understand that you are going through process in his interest. You will often get sympathizers for the politician who will frustrate you. Bureaucrats don't work in their hometowns, and the politician may think you are not for development in his area.

The phrase, "…let him understand that you are going through process in his interest…", summarizes the bureaucratic coping that occurs when bureaucrats face corrupt practices in Ghana's local-government system. While a district may complete a sealed-bid procurement process on paper, it may not be clear if that process accords with the intent of the rules. This bureaucratic coping legitimizes the corruption that infiltrates procurement and other government processes in Ghana. The bureaucrat possesses one advantage over the politician, contractor, and party executive in sealed-bid procurement: she can apply an *imprimatur* of expert discretion to any project or process, which would mask corrupt actions. In choosing a contractor, discretion is necessary because one cannot choose a contractor on cost alone—quality must be considered, and quality is not easily quantifiable. The transaction costs involved in quantifying quality outweigh the benefits of such measurement, especially for seemingly small projects. In short, the bureaucrat controls the discretion required to award contracts. Such discretion can be manipulated to allow bureaucrats (and politicians) to secure private gain from projects. A local bureaucrat's professional discretion and expertise can satisfy the audits of two important constituencies: voters and external donors.

In asking my sample of bureaucrats about these issues, I came to realize that such bureaucratic coping and tacit condoning of corruption was actually an open secret. Many senior bureaucrats admitted that they and their colleagues engaged in such practices—and almost all wished that they did not have to. Most bureaucrats entered the local-government service to serve their country and help their fellow citizens realize better outcomes.

However, it is not easy for internally upstanding bureaucrats to externally protest corrupt actions. In my sample of bureaucrats, almost 40% reported to me that it would not be easy to change corrupt practices in their district. Less than 20% reported that it would be easy to change corrupt practices. For bureaucrats, there are great risks to challenging corrupt practices, especially if such practices are tied to their DCE or other politicians. The greatest such risk, as noted by the bureaucrats in my sample, is that a politician will transfer the bureaucrat out of the district before the bureaucrat's four-year term in the district is complete. Wade (1982) describes how this "transfer mechanism" impacts bureaucrats in India, and Brierley (2019) examines this phenomenon further in Ghana. These political transfers force bureaucrats to move their family to an unknown district (which is already costly) and can be seen as a negative event on their performance records. Approximately half of the bureaucrats I interviewed stated that political transfers occurred either somewhat or very often in the districts in which they had served.

In Massoud's district, many junior officers showed disgruntlement over coping with corruption and threats of political transfer, affirming the actions that Massoud outlined as a senior officer. For these bureaucrats, coping is a norm: they legitimize a corrupted process that ensures funds for politicians and bureaucrats. Though these bureaucrats knowingly legitimize a corrupt system, that system benefits themselves and allows them to handle requests for assistance from family and kin-group members. As a junior planning officer informed me,

> They tell us that we can 'be the change'. But they are using you to cut corners, cheat the system. Over time, public servants who are not inclined to be corrupt are frustrated that they will work 30–40 years and be paupers. [...] The corrupt act is carried out by a syndicate of politicians and bureaucrats—they take the money from the State to use for their families.
>
> The public servants, they know how to cheat the system—a major part of our budget is from the West, and they are becoming aware. [...] They talk about local economic development—even if it comes, it goes to political cronies, the party people! At end of day, money is squandered, but because they are party people you cannot hold them accountable.

This junior planning officer alludes to a key point: bureaucrats serve as a signaling mechanism to donors. If bilateral and multilateral donors, many of whom have financed the training of these bureaucrats, see the bureaucrats' approval, they assume the procurement process was correctly implemented; further, it is simply too costly to investigate procurement in-depth. As a result, donor money ends up being diverted from intended projects. An assistant auditor adds,

> We have procurement procedures—but they've done the thing so many times that it's become a norm. On paper, it looks like the procedure has been followed. Recently, we had to procure new desks, but they jumped straight to the end (of the procurement process). They've repeated it so many times it's a norm. When you want to go by the rules, it becomes difficult because you are just a junior officer.

The corrupted or co-opted bureaucrat weaponizes her technical expertise. Many bureaucrats in Ghana desire to serve their country, and they value their job security. In addition, the bureaucracy is a prestigious institution, which often invites myriad requests for assistance from family and friends. Bureaucrats fear being politically transferred, which not only threatens their job security but also interrupts their ability to meet social obligations and finance their retirements. To cope, bureaucrats must employ their expert discretion to legitimize corrupt political actions, and such discretion can also mask bureaucrats' own illicit activities. Further, bureaucrats must be careful to satisfy politicians of both major parties to ensure that they are not transferred when there is a party change in government.

The contractor

Evans Hayford is a small-scale construction contractor operating in the Upper West region of Ghana. The Upper West is Ghana's newest region, established in 1983, when the Upper Region was divided into Upper West and Upper East. The region is one of the poorest in Ghana, with many infrastructural needs. Upper West lies in the guinea savannah zone, and its major economic activity is agriculture, with millet and shea nut being key crops. Livestock production is also common. Ethnically, the Upper West is home to the Sissala, Wala, and Dagaba ethnic groups. In terms of religion, both Islam and Christianity are widely practiced.

Hayford is a young man, and I receive him and his wife at my hotel in Wa, the regional capital. Hayford completed his primary education in the early 1990s and started work in the oil sector. After a few years managing oil storage and transport, he enrolled in a polytechnic to complete a course in accounting, before returning to Upper West. Due to difficulties in his chosen field, Hayford applied for his contractor license; however, he, like many other contractors in my sample, never indicated that he trained in engineering, construction, quantity surveying, etc. For him, he was motivated by a passion for business. Besides his construction firm, Hayford also manages two other small enterprises. Similar to the vast majority of contractors, his firm is small, though certainly not the smallest in my sample,

> We have basically been operating since 2007, and we construct as demanded: schools, dams and irrigation. In terms of workers, I have seven key workers: superintendent, mason, engineers, etc. For the rest of my labor I depend on temporary staff. On equipment, we lease some and own some; namely, we own a tipper (dump truck), pickup, mixer and leveler.

It is common for construction firms in Ghana to rely on temporary labor, and most companies do not own equipment. Companies tend to be family businesses, and thus they remain small, with only a handful of permanent employees. I asked several contractors why they did not merge to form larger, stronger companies, and many indicated that because of culture most businesses wanted to stay family-run.

Many contractors assert that it is difficult to win contracts through government sealed-bid procurement. These contracts are a contractor's primary source of income, and not winning them presents hardship. The contractors in my sample were all trained in procurement practices by the World Bank and Ghana's Public Procurement Authority, but nearly all argued that winning a bid in Ghana has become a corrupt process.[2] Hayford explains,

> The claims processes at the District Assembly are unnecessary. Go to registry, pay something. Next office, pay something. There are about 10 stages. For district level, it is difficult. You use a lot of money seeing people even before the work starts. [...] You need a 'godfather.' Most of our contractors, 90% of them, are illiterate. How will they get a tax clearance, (social security) certificate, labor clearance?

As Hayford implies, most contractors constructing public works for Ghana's local governments lack the necessary paperwork. Figure 1.1 demonstrates an example Certificate of Classification for a construction contractor in Ghana.

To test whether most contractors working in Ghana had followed official registration procedures, I obtained from the then-Ministry of Water Resources, Works, and Housing a dataset of officially registered contractors in Ghana. In this dataset, there were 5,935 registered Class 3 and Class 4 contractors. Class 3 and Class 4 contractors, the vast majority in Ghana, are small firms with at most a few permanent staff and very little capital equipment. These firms are often engaged

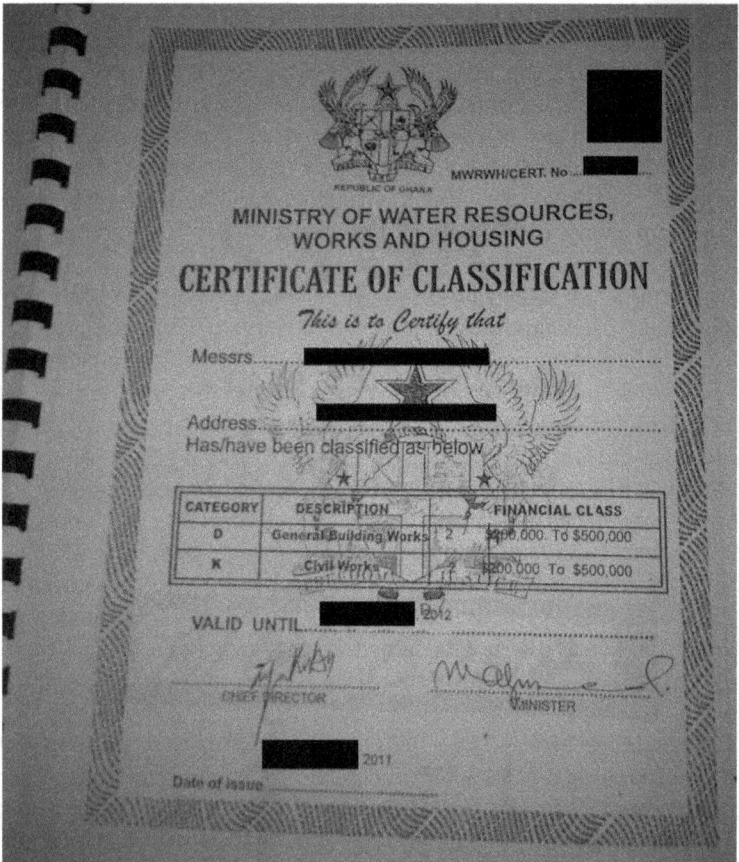

Figure 1.1 Contractor Certificate of Classification.
Source: Author.

by local governments. Class 1 and Class 2 firms in Ghana are larger—sometimes based internationally—and they typically construct complex public works being tendered by the central government. After obtaining data on Ghana's registered contractors, I then collected available data on projects awarded at the district level, specifically looking at districts' annual progress reports for 2012. Ultimately, I collected data on over 7,700 projects reported in 117 district progress reports, out of a then-total of 170 districts.

Under ideal conditions, every construction project in Ghana should be awarded to an officially registered contractor. However, as Table 1.3 demonstrates, in 2012 there was no region of the country where more than 25% of district projects were awarded to officially registered contractors. In seven of ten regions, the plurality of projects was awarded to unregistered contractors. Awarding contracts to unregistered contractors is a clear violation of the procurement law.

Despite these contractors not being registered, how is it that they are winning projects? Hayford, along with many of the other contractors I interviewed, asserts that the procurement process is not fair,

> I felt that in the government sector... I felt that one of the problems... I don't like cheating. It's all about whom you know when you are hiring.

There can be severe penalties for politicians, bureaucrats, and contractors if they are caught cheating the procurement system. Therefore, the potential benefit of cheating the system must be particularly

Table 1.3 Projects Awarded to Certified and Uncertified Contractors by Region, 2012

Region	% Certified	% Uncertified	% Unknown	Sample
All	15.1	51.3	33.7	5028
Ashanti	23.8	69.7	6.6	884
Brong Ahafo	20.3	70.1	9.6	365
Central	10.1	38.6	51.4	765
Eastern	5.3	12.7	82.0	606
Greater Accra	20.1	61.9	18.1	742
Northern	8.6	65.0	26.5	268
Upper East	18.3	81.7	0.0	109
Upper West	2.3	12.6	85.1	302
Volta	11.4	47.9	40.6	463
Western	21.6	67.2	11.3	524

Source: Author's data collection and analysis from official contractor registry and district annual progress reports.

high for these actors to engage in such behavior. Asking Hayford why he felt that contractors needed politicians and politicians needed contractors, he was very clear,

> Politicians need money to do campaign. I am a contractor. He advertises projects. Politician gets project and his money for campaign.
>
> Regional Minister will instruct you that this project is for this contractor, this one for number two... you will not win. [...] They will print four of these documents. Minister will say to you, 'bring your ten percent.' I do that, and he will give me all four documents to make all as correct. You have already met all the people. There are four companies, but they all belong to you.

According to Hayford, procurement corruption helps to finance political campaigns. Hayford affirms, though, that it is not only the politicians who benefit from contractor kickbacks. Public servants also build relationships with contractors. Further, these public servants are lax about monitoring projects; many will not even go to the actual construction sites, but will just look at pictures provided by the contractor.

> They know there is money in it. Public servant wants to build mansion, acquire wife, own a big car. There is a lack of supervision, and shoddy work will come. Fifty thousand of 100,000 (Ghana cedis) is for bribes.

Hayford indicates that he faces many social pressures, just like the politician and the bureaucrat. He also has potentially lucrative access to money, but, the flow of that money can be highly uncertain,

> I can have heart attack. Sister, laborers, steel benders, all these people are coming to you for money. Banks, too. You easily die. Your phone rings, and your heart races. Government will not pay early or at all. You sell property to go and start the work. Will contractors in future be only few? [...] My children will not be contractors.

But are people who enter and stay in construction always interested in political influence? As Hayford indicates, construction has other advantages,

> [Contractors] stay here in Upper West because this region is having the largest amount of construction. This is where (construction)

you can raise the largest amount of capital for other businesses. If I need to build a house, I can use the big money to buy it. [...] Construction is an area where you don't need to be a graduate or Bill Gates to be a contractor. It's just a certificate, and actually you don't really need that. The industry is not bad, but government makes it bad.

Given poor educational quality in much of Ghana, many students do not matriculate to the polytechnic or tertiary levels, levels which might allow them to enter various professions. Construction has a low barrier to entry, and very little is required to start a firm, which makes construction an attractive industry. In addition, many Ghanaians want to head their own business, but it is difficult to borrow starting funds when banking institutions are scarce (or charge high interest) and when one has little collateral. Construction, in which money may come from the state in the form of large contracts, provides one method of raising funds to start a business or finance someone else's business. For contractors in a developing country, the most significant challenge is simply to win contracts. Politicians and bureaucrats control the contract-awarding process, so contractors must effectively signal their loyalty to these gatekeepers.

The party chair

Alhaji Yakubu is an NDC regional chairman. Interviewing regional chairs could present challenges; frequently, I was referred to a regional secretary or organizer (still high-ranking positions) because the chair was too busy or was not conversant enough in English. It was a common theme, with both major parties, for chairs to be relatively less educated and contractors by profession, while other senior officers were teachers with more education.

Yakubu resembled Plunkitt of Tammany Hall (Riordon 1905). The interview itself was literally a bumpy experience, as it occurred in his car as he darted around his regional capital for meetings. These meetings were varied, and we stopped at the Regional Minister's office, a local polytechnic, various consultants' offices, and other locations.

Yakubu proudly states that he never went to school and that he joined the NDC in the early 1990s, around the time when he started his construction firm. Yakubu rose through the party ranks quickly, and has held the regional chairmanship for many years. His firm constructs buildings, roads, and dormitories, and has even constructed offices for district assemblies. On asking him about his duties as a regional party chair, Yakubu first states,

> Because my party is in power, I help my people. When I win the election, I'll help people with funerals, weddings, etc.

Helping one's "people" is the most important duty for a regional party chair. Similar to politicians, there are many requests from people for financial assistance, especially when it comes to funerals, which are major social events in Ghana. As an NPP party official in Yakubu's region informed me, "Politics starts at the funeral home". I have even heard of constituency party officials racing to transport a dead body in their party's pickup truck. As a party chair, Yakubu must rely on party operatives—known in Ghana as "foot soldiers"—to campaign in rural areas for the party's candidates. After fulfilling their service, these foot soldiers turn to party chairs for assistance. I ask Yakubu about the most common requests he receives,

> People want help to get government jobs, especially teaching and employment at the various assemblies and ministries. Some boys will come here asking about school fees—university, secondary, primary.
>
> As for my relationship with contractors, when jobs come up here, I help them so they have something to eat.

These realities are affirmed by senior party officers in other parts of Ghana,

> I employ sympathizers of the Party, so they will be rewarded. I help the Party ... We don't take salary from the Party. But being in government, you know some people and you can ask for work, can ask for contracts.
>
> [Party redacted] Regional Organizer, Transitional Zone

Yakubu emphasized his role as a social connector, and it played out as we drove around the regional capital, with him dropping off envelopes and picking others up. We were also frequently interrupted by his mobile phone, and he explained to me that contractors were calling him about various issues. He emphasized his role as a connector for politicians, contractors, and other important persons,

> When the districts have problems, the DCE tells me, and I tell the Minister and the party people.

While it would not be unexpected for a DCE to report directly to a Minister, it seems unexpected that a party chair would highlight his role as a medium between a DCE and the Regional Minister. Why should a Regional Minister care about the party chair? As several party officials pointed out to me, Regional Ministers are often less powerful than their respective region's party chair. Each Regional Minister owes his nomination and position, and maybe even the financing of his campaign, to the regional chair. Every Regional Minister knows that he was brought in by the regional party chair—and he knows that the regional party chair can just as easily bring someone else in. As one regional party officer recounted to me,

> Up to [year redacted], we had difficulties with the Regional Minister. He did not understand the game of politics, and we stood up. He should know that it is the Party that brought him to government. Party is a check on him, and there is a manifesto to implement.
> [Party redacted] Regional Treasurer, Savannah Zone

As politicians rise, they need more money to win. This is true for MPs and Regional Ministers, and they ultimately are beholden to their Party's support. According to Yakubu,

> With the MPs, our relationship is good. I helped many of them to win—we assisted by buying [motorcycles] and giving out cash. I would also talk to the people.

Political-party chairs prefer that their chosen candidates win elections. Even before the primary stage, political aspirants are vetted by party chairs, who can determine whether those aspirants progress to the next stage. Similar to politicians, party chairs serve their local constituents, but their preferred candidates must win. Once those candidates win, they "owe" a party chair for his support.

As a result, Yakubu is in a position of great power. He is instrumental to the fortunes and ambitions of politicians and contractors. Being a rich contractor himself, he can assist many people and demand favors in return. He can help less fortunate contractors find wealth. For a regional chair to continue executing his duties, he must satisfy the myriad demands of the foot soldiers who support him and ensure the loyalty of regional politicians in his party. A regional chair's most difficult task is ensuring that he has sufficient sources of income to maintain his position and prevent challengers from campaigning against him.

Notes

1 For a literary discussion, see Achebe (1960).
2 In researching this book, the author found contractors to interview through the attendance lists of World Bank-sponsored procurement workshops.

References

Achebe, Chinua. 1960. *No Longer at Ease.* London: Heinemann.
Brierley, Sarah. 2019. "Unprincipled Principals: Co-opted Bureaucrats and Corruption in Ghana." *American Journal of Political Science,* Forthcoming. URL: https://www.sarahbrierley.com/research.html
Government of Ghana. 2003. *Act 663: Public Procurement Act.* URL: https://www.ppaghana.org/documents/Public%20Procurement%20Act%20 2003%20Act%20663.pdf
Riordon, William. 1905. *Plunkitt of Tammany Hall: A Series of Very Plain Talks on Very Practical Politics.* New York, NY: McClure, Phillips & Co.
Schlesinger, Joseph. 1966. *Ambition and Politics: Political Careers in the United States.* Chicago, IL: Rand McNally.
Wade, Robert. 1982. "The System of Administrative and Political Corruption: Canal Irrigation in South India." *The Journal of Development Studies,* 18(3): 287–328.

2 The iron square of political finance

The allocation of money is the water that nourishes and connects the motivations of the four players in the political ecosystem. A politician can have progressive ambitions, but she must finance her campaigns to win elections. However, whom a politician owes, defines how she will behave. Bureaucrats value job security and serving Ghana; but almost all face social pressures to assist family and save for their own retirements. Contractors are driven to succeed financially in their industry—an industry in which government is the largest client by a significant margin. Party chairs are political power brokers: they groom and finance new candidates, but they must also reward their hard-working party operatives.

There are many ways in which politicians, bureaucrats, contractors, and party chairs can extract money from citizens and the state. These players could demand bribes directly from citizens. Some do, but this is a very visible, tiresome form of corruption that can lead to arrest or negative publicity. Political parties could levy higher membership dues to raise revenue, but numerous respondents informed me that citizens, many of whom are living near the subsistence margin, rarely pay dues, and there is little ability to enforce dues payment. Money could be outright stolen from citizens and businesses, but such actions are likely to incur social unrest and other costs.

Local-development funds at district assemblies are an attractive source of money for local politicians, bureaucrats, contractors, and party chairs. Districts receive funds from three sources: internal generation, central government, and donors. Internally generated funds, which are raised from property taxes and small penalties imposed on citizens, are the smallest sources of revenue for most districts, typically less than 20% of a district's budget. Urban districts such as Accra, however, generate higher amounts of internal funds. Central-government funds account for the largest share of district resources. As Table 2.1 demonstrates, in

Table 2.1 District Assemblies Common Fund Disbursements (2012) by Region

Region	Number of Districts	Amount (Ghana Cedis)
All	216	190,579,357.48
Ashanti	30	23,503,088.08
Brong Ahafo	27	20,633,051.54
Central	20	14,736,521.13
Eastern	26	18,173,010.74
Greater Accra	16	41,493,476.76
Northern	26	20,549,983.81
Upper East	13	9,273,761.26
Upper West	11	8,508,659.73
Volta	25	17,612,540.32
Western	22	16,095,264.11

Source: District Assemblies Common Fund Quarterly Press Releases, 2012.

2012, the Government of Ghana transferred over 190 million Ghana cedis (around US$125 million at the time of this study) to its 216 districts through the District Assemblies Common Fund (DACF) (DACF 2012).[1] Similarly, foreign donors contributed 473.4 million Ghana cedis from 2006 to 2011 through the District Development Facility (DDF) (The Chronicle 2014). Due to Ghana's decentralized government system, once funds from the DACF and DDF are allocated to a district, the district controls how these funds are used in procuring public works.

The Public Procurement Act

To extract resources while minimizing the possibility of prosecution, the four players take advantage of district-level procurement. When a district in Ghana needs to provide public goods, they are required to adhere to the Public Procurement Act of 2003 (Act 663). I describe three critical features of Act 663: membership of procurement entities, procurement regulations, and procurement procedures.

Every district in Ghana is required to have a District Tender Committee as well as a District Tender Review Board. The District Tender Committee is the body that actually facilitates procurement of public goods and works, and it is headed by the District Chief Executive (DCE). Other members include the District Finance Officer, a lawyer appointed by the District Assembly, one Member of Parliament (MP), and three department heads, such as the District Engineer or the District Education Officer. The committee secretary is the District Coordinating Director (DCD). In terms of accountability, a district's

Tender Review Board is charged with overseeing the actions of the District Tender Committee. Its membership is drawn from the legislators of the District Assembly, and their secretary is the District Planning Officer. In short, these are the people who make local development happen.

Act 663 details numerous procurement regulations. According to the Act, a District Tender Committee can award projects valued up to 50,000 Ghana cedis, approximately US$32,000 at the time of this study. However, provision 17-2(c) of the Act also specifies that the District Tender Committee can award contracts valued up to 200,000 Ghana cedis, as long as it has the approval of the Tender Review Board. The Act specifies these exact amounts, rather than percentages of the local development budget. Due to inflation, many districts face the challenge of awarding projects at costs below these thresholds, and there has been little Parliamentary action to correct this oversight. To qualify for public contracts, contractors are required to possess professional and technical qualifications; an official Certificate of Classification from the then-Ministry of Water Resources, Works, and Housing; financial resources; equipment; managers; and personnel. Districts typically award projects according to National Competitive Tendering, in which only Ghanaian firms that meet technical requirements are allowed to bid.

To solicit bidders for projects, District Tender Committees are required to follow a strict procedure. Districts advertise an "Invitation for Tenders" in at least two nationally distributed newspapers, detailing the requirements contractors must meet as well as a deadline by which contractors must submit their sealed bidding documents. At the appointed date, bidding documents are opened by the District Tender Committee in the presence of bidders that wish to attend. At this meeting, each bidder's bid price will be announced, as well as whether they included the appropriate documents in their bid. The Tender Committee is then required to determine whether bidders are "responsive"— that is, they meet the requirements specified in the advertisement—or whether they are "non-responsive" or "non-performing". If the bidders fall into the latter category, the bids are thrown out. After opening the bids, technical experts (usually the District Planning Officer, District Engineer, and others) will—in theory—scrutinize the bids to ensure bidders are qualified, before formalizing the project award to the qualified bidder with the lowest price.

Despite its detailed requirements, Act 663 contains numerous provisions that can be abused. For instance, if a contractor's bid is rejected, under section 29-2, the district is not required to provide justification for the bid's rejection. Such a provision can allow members of the tender committee to selectively enforce rules.[2] While a district is supposed to ensure that contractors are qualified and that these qualifications are noted in tender advertisements, section 59-2 states that no criterion that is not included in the tender invitation can be used against a bidder.

While the procurement law clearly lists criteria that must be met to ensure that bidding is fair, in practice, the process is subject to human motivations. I observed a tender opening meeting in one sample district that was not carried out according to the Public Procurement Act, and I describe the event here.

District X bid openings

The friendly agricultural officer of District X ushered me into the DCE's office, showing me to the large conference table. I greeted the education officer and district planner, both of whom I had already interviewed. The education officer was affable and gregarious, as usual, but the planning officer seemed sullen. At the other side of the DCE's office sat a half-dozen men, silent and bored. Gradually, junior officers arrived to record minutes, until eight of us were present around the conference table.

The DCE and DCD arrived and took their places. The DCE appeared nervous, barely greeting us. Throughout the meeting his phone would ring, and he would step out to take the calls privately. Soon after, the District Engineer and his junior engineers arrived, struggling to carry a large wooden box—the District Tender Box. Today, District X was opening sealed bids from contractors bidding on district projects. While contractors are mandated to drop bids into the box by an appointed time, earlier that morning I witnessed one man drop several bids into the box after the deadline.

This district's protocol dictates that the Engineer leads the opening, taking each sealed bid envelope out of the tender box and reading off the cost figures that sum to the total bid amount. This Engineer read the bids in halting fashion. He failed to announce certain amounts. He took too long in between each bid. It was clear he did not know what he was doing.

For those of us at the table, we were given "bid evaluation forms". Figure 2.1 presents one such bid evaluation form. On each form was a grid corresponding to a particular project for which a contract was to be awarded. On that day, eight contracts were to be awarded, ranging from schools to latrines to market stalls. In each box of the evaluation

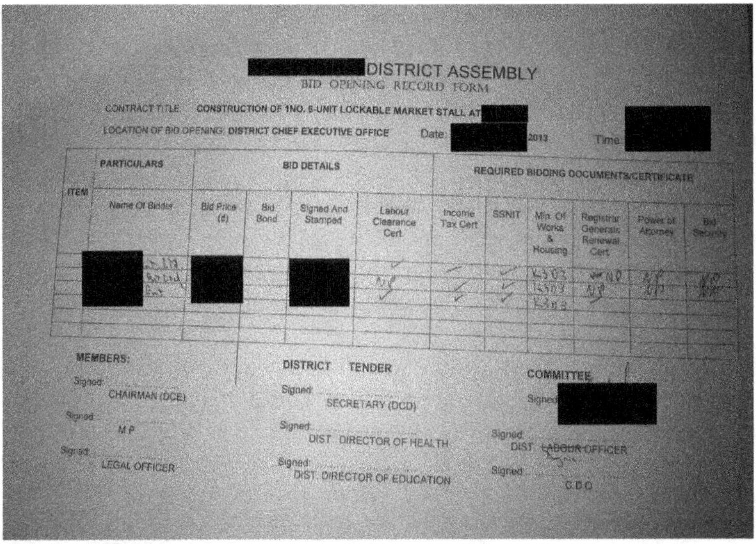

Figure 2.1 Example Bid Opening Record Form.
Source: Author.

form, we filled in the appropriate number when the Engineer would read out an estimated cost figure, or we would check whether certain criteria were met, such as the official contractor-qualification licenses being included with the bid. After each project, we passed our sheets around the table and affixed our signatures, signifying that the process had met our approval and was conducted legally. One officer noted that the Engineer was failing to read estimates for certain bids, but the DCD reassured the group,

> Oh, we forgot to include some of those criteria—bid bonds; power of attorney; and bid security—in the main advert[isement], so we cannot hold the bidders to those criteria. We will be sure to include those things later.

Given that all contractors in Ghana eligible for public projects are required to have these materials, it is certainly strange that the DCD would simply waive them. Districts tender new projects approximately every quarter, so it should not be difficult for bureaucrats—especially experienced bureaucrats—to have an advertisement template that already includes these criteria. There are a few anomalies in Figure 2.1 that should be noted. There are only three bidders for this project—which was the case for most projects discussed that day. Of those three bidders, those on the first two lines have several boxes marked, "NP", which stands for non-performing. In other words, those bidders are missing components of their bid package and would thus be disqualified. As a result, only one bidder would even be qualified to win this project.

As more and more project bids were opened, the planning officer's demeanor transformed from nonchalant to concerned to agitated. He knew that procedures were not being followed. He knew that other bureaucrats were being purposefully silent. He knew that coincidences were not coincidental. Finally, reaching his limit, he exclaimed,

> What are we doing?! Why are there always only three bidders? Why are these project amounts all above 50,000 cedis? The law limits us to 50,000 cedis! This is not right.

The room went silent. Everyone stared the planning officer down. A junior officer smirked, rolling her eyes. What this planner had exclaimed was an open secret, and similar such stories were recounted to me by numerous other bureaucrats outside this particular district. Many projects have only three bidders, though, in a competitive system, there could theoretically be many more. But, because of the threat of political transfers and other sanctions, most bureaucrats fear speaking out against this system. Breaking the silence, the DCE returns fire,

> No! The limit is 200,000! Or is it 100,000?

This exchange highlighted the law's ambiguity about contract thresholds for District Tender Committees and District Tender Review Boards. During this argument, the Engineer suggested another figure (which was still wrong), and the DCD rushed to calm everyone down as other bureaucrats concurred with the planning officer. Several officers even brought out the actual procurement law. The tender meeting descended into chaos, with several officers pointing fingers at each other. After a few minutes, the education officer calmly restored order,

> As long as the auditors see that we have all signed the documents, they won't mind.

With that, the remaining bureaucrats and DCE fell in to line. Essentially, the education officer described the *imprimatur* of bureaucratic expertise.

As long as the District Tender Committee signed their evaluation sheets, the auditors would believe (or at least have plausible deniability) that the bureaucrats supervised the procurement process with integrity. Throughout the meeting, the men on the other side of the room sat unperturbed.

Following the tender-board meeting, I returned to my guesthouse to type notes. I received a call from a junior officer who attended the meeting, requesting to meet over drinks. I asked his opinion of the day's meeting,

> We have thieves in this country who steal by the roadside. But the public servants, they steal with their pens.

This tender-board meeting—like most others—was not open to the public. As a result, Ghanaian citizens and outside donors may have little idea about how contracts are actually awarded—"stealing with their pens" is, unlike many forms of petty corruption, a well-cloaked form of corruption. However, the eight projects up for tendering at this meeting were each valued at approximately $20,000, so the financial returns are much higher compared to, say, paying bribes to a traffic officer. I term this level of corruption, "mid-level corruption"—larger than petty corruption, but smaller than "grand corruption" that is seen with national-level privatizations and other similar projects. In my sample of districts, mid-level corruption of the procurement process was reported to me by almost all bureaucrats interviewed. Unfortunately, though such corruption has relatively high financial stakes, there is less incentive for the media to investigate and detail these stories compared to grand corruption.

It was still unclear to me why the bureaucrats assented so easily after the education officer commented about their signatures. This junior officer had a ready explanation,

> Once you are a director, you can be having your own companies, awarding contracts to yourself. You are both judge and jury.

In other words, each of these bureaucrats may have had a financial interest in the outcomes of the day's tender openings. For bureaucrats, wages are low, and they must supplement their income to meet social demands and save for retirement. These bureaucrats face numerous societal pressures and have few means to meet them. The junior officer also explained why the planning officer was treated so harshly by the DCE and other bureaucrats,

But if you criticize someone, they will take it as a personal attack! If you keep making noise, they will insult you—maybe not to your face, but behind your back. One day you may travel away from the town and find yourself transferred.

Many respondents expressed a fear of being insulted by their colleagues, which greatly hampers efforts to correct corrupt behavior. This junior officer also affirmed the threat of political transfers, which are not only costly to an ousted bureaucrat but also disrupt secondary income streams (e.g., construction firms owned on the side) that he may be using to meet social obligations and save for retirement. Thus, bureaucrats are caught in a dilemma. However, I was still puzzled about the presence of the other men in the room. The junior officer answered,

Those men there, they were contractors and party boys. But they already knew the outcome.

This comment was enlightening. Politicians, bureaucrats, contractors, and party chairs were all represented at the tender opening, and they were all connected. The process was rigged, and it benefited all of them. In Ghana, politicians, bureaucrats, contractors, and party chairs are critical figures in providing (or not providing) public goods. It should be noted that the dynamics described above were reaffirmed in all 11 districts of my sample—not one refuted these behaviors. Why is individual opposition—as evidenced by the District Planning Officer in the meeting above—not more successful? And why does Ghanaian society even permit these players to come together and act in this way?

A theory of political finance

From the perspective of politicians, bureaucrats, contractors, and party chairs, the use of procurement corruption to finance political activities is rational: what is expected from each player is sustained by what is expected from the other players. In Ghana, the political system starts at the village, and, for decades, local parties have been central to Ghanaians' lives (Apter 1955; Hodgkin 1961). When citizens need food, payment of hospital bills, or funeral funds for a deceased loved one, they turn to their local party leaders for help—and, because of intermarriage and family ties across parties, it does not matter which party. These party leaders are villagers, themselves, and are attuned to the needs of their fellow citizens—but they also expect the support of these citizens during elections. Party leaders I interviewed emphasized the importance of their social obligations and the village-level camaraderie and reciprocity that exists across party lines. These local parties are providers for many.

Meeting the needs of fellow villagers is a costly task. Party leaders stretch meager funds to meet requests, but ultimately the requests become too expensive, such as demands to build a new school. At this point, winning political office, and accessing the funds of central government, becomes paramount. Politicians arise from the local levels and there are numerous offices to fill, which would allow them to contribute to their communities (Weber 1946; Schlesinger 1966). These politicians can channel the funds needed to build a new school. However, political campaigns are expensive, requiring significant travel, advertisements, and a support staff. How does a candidate find the means to campaign and win office? Even if it is observed that political candidates extract funds from procurement corruption, how does such a system sustain and enforce itself, despite efforts to combat corruption? The answers to these questions are the sparks that ignite a political machine (Scott 1969).

Extraction

I will assume that Ghanaian politicians prefer to win elections. Winning elections is the initial threshold that politicians must meet to address their other interests, such as serving constituents. To win elections, though, a Ghanaian politician must satisfy the material needs of her constituents (Asante & Kunnath 2018). These social pressures for private benefits detract from a politician's ability to legislate or provide public goods (Lindberg 2010). Ignoring the demands of one's constituents, however, could result in a candidate losing the next primary. Almost all politicians in my sample lamented constituent requests as a heavy burden of office.

> That one is terrible! They come in as early as 4AM on phone. Some come to Parliament with social issues, school fees, funerals, marriage, outdoorings, harvests. All manners of people: some want employment with police and security. They look at you as their lord. If you don't pick it (the phone), there is a problem.
>
> MP, New Patriotic Party

From the moment a citizen decides to run for political office, she must raise money. Some citizens possess enough wealth to finance their campaigns (Asante & Kunnath 2018), but a political campaign is a gamble that could lead to substantial losses or lucrative gains. After ensuring that she has popular support, the candidate seeks donors.

> Most don't fund campaign alone: friends, relatives, contractors— not just loans (from the bank). There are expectations. If you want to go to Parliament, if from a district, most rich people will assist you. If you can become Minister, you can help them get contracts.
> (Regional Party Secretary, National Democratic Congress)

In Ghana, a political aspirant can borrow money from local contractors to finance her first campaign. There is no shortage of small contractors, with over 5,000 officially registered and countless others not registered. These borrowed funds can be used to attract primary and general-election voters with private benefits or outright vote buying. In exchange, the political candidate promises to repay her financial backers with contracts should she win office. Campaigns, especially with vote buying, are expensive. In January 2014, the Majority Leader of the Parliament of Ghana stated that each MP in the House owes at least 300,000 Ghana cedis to private banks for their campaigns (Fordjuor 2014). According to Asante and Kunnath (2018), parliamentary candidates needed, on average, 389,803 Ghana cedis to contest the 2016 parliamentary elections; in 2012, candidates needed 245,615 Ghana cedis, on average. At the time of this study, parliamentarians' salaries were around 70,000 Ghana cedis annually.[3] DCEs receive smaller salaries, but they are also responsible for meeting constituents' demands for private goods.

District-level procurement provides contractors with the funds by which they can finance political candidates. Several times per year, districts advertise "Calls for Tender" in the national newspapers, inviting contractors to bid for such projects as schools, clinics, and rural roads.[4] Contractors submit their sealed bid packets to the district, usually within a month of the advertisement's posting. On the deadline date, the DCE meets with her senior bureaucrats (DCD, District Finance Officer, etc.) to open the sealed bids. Bidders are nominally required to submit numerous documents with their bid amounts, such as their contractor registration, labor certificate, and social-security forms.

Following the bid-opening meeting, senior bureaucrats convene for two weeks to conduct a "tender review process" to determine the contractors' quality. A contractor cannot simply submit a low-priced bid, assuming she will win the contract. The procurement law allows for bureaucrats to evaluate contractors and choose a higher-priced contractor if they believe she will do a better job. In theory, such discretion should lead to better contractors chosen, but, in practice, it affords significant latitude for malfeasance.

Bureaucratic discretion is central to procurement. Because bureaucrats are technical experts and are empowered by the procurement law to assess contractor quality, their *imprimatur* is a signal to outsiders (namely, auditors) that the selected contractor has been properly vetted. As a result, politicians need the bureaucrats' cooperation to ensure legal protection, and the politicians can exploit the bureaucrats' desire to retire comfortably and meet social expectations to gain that cooperation. Politicians allow bureaucrats to claim projects as "theirs" and extract kickbacks from contractors building district projects—these kickbacks amply supplement bureaucrats' salaries. At the time of this study, district-level projects in Ghana were valued at around 50,000 Ghana cedis. Ensminger (2017) describes similar behavior in Kenya, where officials with high levels of discretion pick projects with kickback opportunities despite differing community needs. David-Barrett and Fazekas (2019) note that, in Hungary, politicians can influence who is selected to be procurement advisors within a bureaucratic agency, which can then lead to contracts being channeled to politically connected companies.

To illustrate this arrangement between politicians and bureaucrats, I employ a visual example from a district assembly. In Figure 2.2, a district is awarding six projects, shown on the left side. The DCE

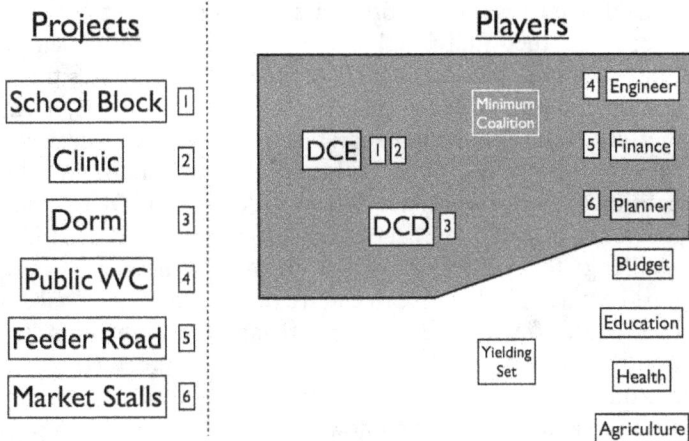

Figure 2.2 DCE Allocating Projects to Bureaucrats.
Source: Author.

has chosen the school and clinic projects for her own contractors. The DCD, the district's bureaucratic head, has chosen the dormitory project for her own contractors. Other bureaucrats (Engineer, Finance Officer, and Planner) receive a single project. The remaining officers are left out of this procurement round (the "yielding set"). A minimum coalition of the DCE and several bureaucrats is sufficient to ensure that the procurement process is validated, but small enough to maximize winnings for each participant. In other words, a sufficient number of bureaucrats are pacified through kickback opportunities to ensure that all of the projects are approved, but there are not enough disgruntled bureaucrats to overthrow the process. These disgruntled bureaucrats know that they can wait for a later tender meeting to reap benefits, eventually becoming senior enough to reap benefits more frequently.

DCEs are playing an ultimatum game with bureaucrats.[5] The DCE offers a selection of projects to bureaucrats; if enough bureaucrats are satisfied with the offer, then the DCE and that group of bureaucrats get to "claim" those projects for themselves (and their affiliated contractors). In theory, DCEs should not have to share projects with bureaucrats, because bureaucrats are no worse off if they received no projects (and, by law, they are not supposed to receive any). However, if enough bureaucrats believe a DCE has treated them unfairly, they can reject the projects and work to oust the DCE, harming all parties, since then no one may get projects. Though bureaucrats are aware of the procurement regulations, they are caught in a collective-action problem. They could band together to prevent such procurement corruption, but, in practice, their individual incentive to save for retirement overrides coordination. Any individual bureaucrat that opposes this process could simply be excluded from the tender negotiations, harming only herself as her fellow bureaucrats take her share of projects. In subsequent procurement rounds, other bureaucrats can be included in the coalition to ensure continued collective complicity. DCEs condone this process to maintain bureaucrats' favor in the future. Bureaucrats who challenge this process—like the Planning Officer from District X—must be particularly brave to endure the potential personal costs.

A contractor offers kickbacks to politicians and bureaucrats to ensure that he will be favored during project procurement. (In practice, though, only a select number of contractors will bid because those without the right connections know they will not win.) Typically, a kickback amounts to 10% of the contract value. The negotiations between contractors, bureaucrats, and politicians occur informally, such as through phone or text message, outside of official records.

Such messages would be almost impossible for whistleblowers or auditors to trace. Respondents often referred to kickbacks as a "thank you" exchanged between participants; such behavior, though corrupt, has been embedded as a social norm. For bureaucrats, the kickback provides the funds for retirement. For politicians, the kickback finances campaigns.

> Before you tender, make sure you have all arrangements set. Here, I get in touch with [DCE], DPO, DBO, etc. They have to know you well. If there is a tender, and you don't do your homework, you lose.
>
> Contractor, District H

As the contractor in District H points out, a contractor needs to arrange with bureaucrats that they will "win" a project. The contractor then has to actually submit a bid (or several bids), though she knows that she will win a certain project; submitting the bids is a safeguard in case of an audit, especially from donors. However, the procurement rules must still nominally be followed. In my data gathering on district contracts, I observed that contractors practiced rotational bidding, where out of, say, three contractors bidding on three projects, those contractors would rotate who "won" a given project. Some bidders who were "non-performing" when bidding for a particular project happened to have all their documents when bidding for another project.

For contractors to realize profits they construct shoddily. Many contractors reported to me that between 30% and 50% of a contract award could be expended on kickbacks alone, since those kickbacks are usually paid to multiple people. There is an ultimatum game between contractors and bureaucrats; in theory, contractors should not have to give any kickbacks to bureaucrats, who are no worse for not receiving kickbacks. However, such kickbacks are viewed as a "thank you" norm, and bureaucrats can blacklist contractors who do not provide kickbacks. Contractors are themselves caught in a collective-action problem; individually, they know that they should not pay kickbacks to bureaucrats, but any individual who openly opposes the system will be ostracized, and therefore lose this critical income stream.

There are other financial challenges for contractors. Ghana suffers from periods of rapid inflation, which hamper a contractor's ability to purchase materials. The distribution of funds from the district government to the contractor can be severely delayed, and contractors reported that they could wait up to four years for payment. Many contractors used fewer bags of cement than required or adjusted building plans to account for bribes and delayed payments. The result is that structures often fail within a few years. However, such politically induced obsolescence provides opportunity for future rent extraction in the form of rehabilitation projects or new projects altogether.

Enforcement

While politicians must finance campaigns and bureaucrats must finance retirements, these needs alone are not sufficient to maintain the system. A set of politicians could coordinate to reform political finance or a large-enough set of bureaucrats could expose these actions. I argue that political parties, namely their executives, are central to enforcing the stability of this political-finance arrangement. Party chairs are powerful interlocutors in a candidate's political fortunes, and these chairs often vet prospective candidates before primary elections.

Party chairs mobilize the activists and voters that a candidate needs to win. At the village level, these activists—popularly known as "foot soldiers"—turn out votes for the party. Chairs oversee these foot soldiers and maintain good personal relations with them. In exchange for their support, foot soldiers expect material benefits from their party chairs. In interviews, most party chairs emphasized their personal relationships with the foot soldiers: attending family funerals, supporting children's events, paying medical bills, etc.

> You see, it was the party that got you into power, whether you are the President or an MP. In the Party, we have what are called 'foot soldiers'. They go into the very rural, remote areas, and they canvas for votes. They go places where President and MPs cannot go. That is why they are important, and that is why Accra listens to them.
>
> DCE, District F

> That is very, very true. With the subletting (subcontracting), some of the party activists, we call them 'foot soldiers', win, but they have no certificates or skills. What happens when contract is given to them? They sublet it … party activists get this money and share amongst themselves.
>
> Contractor, District D

To win the favor of politicians and party chairs, some contractors join the ranks of foot soldiers (Ninsin 2006; Bob-Milliar 2012). These foot soldiers canvas rural areas to raise money and turn out votes, often through their kinship and ethnic networks, particularly in areas where the party may be electorally weak. In exchange for their services, foot soldiers demand "selective incentives" (Whiteley & Seyd 2002) in the form of personal support and project contracts. The most lucrative selective incentives are bestowed upon foot soldiers who have devoted significant time and money to improving the party's standing in a given area, and foot soldiers compete against each other for such incentives (Bob-Milliar 2012). Foot soldiers face significant risk, though: a party can still lose the national elections, which would hamper the party's ability to distribute selective incentives, thus endangering the foot soldiers' survival.

Chairs maintain the loyalty of foot soldiers through their connections and control over contracts and kickbacks—similar to the functioning of political machines in American political history (Riordon 1905). While contracts are nominally controlled by district governments, occasionally, larger contracts are distributed to regions from Accra. At each level, party chairs distribute contracts to loyal contractors as well as themselves. How are regional chairs able to influence the distribution of these contracts? Essentially, the tacit approval for this arrangement stems from the top: regional chairs influence presidential elections through their relationship with the foot soldiers, many of whom are voting delegates at presidential nominating conventions. Bob-Milliar (2012) notes the prevalence of factionalism in Ghana's major political parties; party chairs and executives play important roles in supporting factions and negotiating between them. At party conventions,

> The regional chair plays a big role. As a regional boss, it is expected that you have control over your constituents, your delegates. Once a regional chair, you have control. Delegates come from the constituency, and they respect your views. Candidates invite you and talk to you. You have control, managerial control.
>
> Former Regional Chairman, National Democratic Congress

> By Constitution, we need to be fair officers. We are humans, though. Four [presidential candidates] stood in front, and definitely you like one. You give every candidate a chance. If you have a choice, you work behind the scenes for that choice. But, still, be a father to all.
>
> Former Regional Chairman, National Democratic Congress

Each party has ten regional chairs (one for each region), who oversee legions of supporters. During presidential primaries, regional chairs can ensure that favored candidates win the nomination with the support of loyalists in their region. Ghana's party chairs, like political brokers and bosses around the world, frequently work behind the scenes to ensure support for particular candidates. As a result, even a President of Ghana owes regional chairs for their support. Regional chairs have the power to recommend to the President potential DCEs, Cabinet Ministers, and Regional Ministers, all of whom would owe regional chairs for their support. This dynamic further strengthens the political power of party chairs. These savvy chairs are then favored for large regional contracts,

> As a typical example, in [location redacted] the Regional Minister awarded three new senior high schools… In each [senior high school], Chair has two projects. Regional Minister started a library project; money was too huge, and library was not pre-financed. The Regional Minister wanted competent contractors, but the Regional Chair wanted the contract—he even went to Accra. The Regional Chair engaged sole bidder, that is, selling the contracts to someone who gets all the bid documents. The Chair took 10 percent.
>
> Constituency Secretary, [Party Redacted]

> The Minister and Regional Party Chair can take up to 30 or 40 contracts and share with any party supporters. The parties are financed by individuals, and if the party comes to power, they get back their money and have opportunities at many things. They will even get more than 100x return on party finance.
>
> Contractor, District B

Party chairs have exploited a vicious cycle of money in politics: their position in power allows them to accrue wealth, and that accrual of wealth allows them to gain more power. They gain power via their positions as "kingmakers" for candidates seeking higher office. Should a President fail to adhere to his chairs' recommendations, the chairs possess a credible threat of using their political and financial power to destabilize regional capitals and support other candidates in the next Presidential primaries.

Because a party chair can thus influence contracts and control foot soldiers, an incumbent politician or political aspirant must signal their loyalty to the party chair. Typically this loyalty entails the promise of contract kickbacks, whether for the chair herself or for the chair's associates. Such action shows that the politician is "committed" to the party, and these kickbacks allow the chair to reward foot soldiers. MPs, in particular, complained about this equilibrium. They argue that they should be allowed to perform their national-level duties rather than be local development agents, but they are compelled to satisfy the demands of their local party executives and constituents if they wish to be reelected—and have any chance of carrying out the agendas that inspired them to politics in the first place.

Regional party chairs hold significant power over the politicians in their region, and Figure 2.3 depicts the interactions between chairs and politicians. In a given region, a party chair "oversees" multiple politicians—that is, those politicians are indebted to the chair for his electoral support. Each chair can mobilize foot soldiers to support these politicians during election periods (depicted by the arrows towards the politicians in Figure 2.3). In exchange, foot soldiers expect chairs to provide for them and maintain good relations. Chairs finance these relationships through the kickbacks received from the politicians in her region (depicted by the arrows from the politicians to the chair), who are themselves extracting funds from the contractors building the projects.

Politicians are playing ultimatum games with regional party chairs. Legally, politicians should not be exchanging kickbacks for chairs' support; in theory, chairs would not be made worse off. However, chairs possess the credible threat of mobilizing foot soldiers against a politician if the politician fails to provide sufficient funds. As a result, politicians pay the chairs. Politicians need the support of chairs to

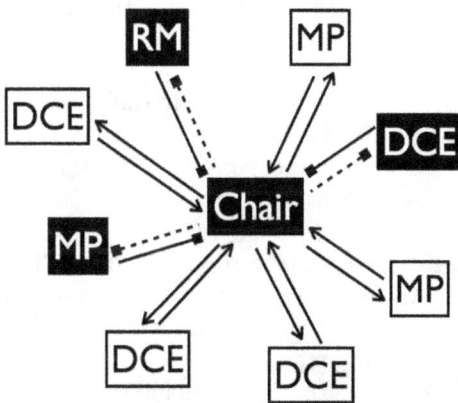

Figure 2.3 Regional Chairs, Politicians, and Political Support.
Source: Author.

maintain their own standing and accomplish political goals. If a chair becomes upset, that politician's career could be over. There are many other unsuspecting candidates who are ready to play these games.

Though politicians know that this arrangement is detrimental to their careers and ability to serve the public, they are caught in a collective-action problem. It would take a critical mass of politicians to stop funding a chair over several procurement cycles to disable the credible threat of chairs mobilizing foot soldiers against a politician. However, it would be in each politician's individual interest to defect from such coordination by continuing to pay the chair and avoid conflict. A chair who mobilizes foot soldiers against a politician can inflict electoral defeat—and ensure a more "loyal" candidate wins in the next election. In Figure 2.3, the Regional Minister, a DCE, and an MP (depicted in black boxes) failed to supply enough money, and foot soldiers were sent to destabilize those politicians (depicted by dashed lines).

> The Regional Chair mobilized youth and they vandalized the Regional Coordinating Council. They destroyed the tender box. The Regional Chair has all the projects in this region, but only one project is executed by himself. They give these out on percentage basis. They become a party chairman to enrich themselves.
> Constituency Party Secretary, National Democratic Congress

The party chair's control of the foot soldiers compels politicians to steal funds from the procurement process. The chair's pressure on the politician is transferred to bureaucrats and contractors to ensure funds are extracted from procurement.

> The pressure transcends from DCE to staff. You transfer it to staff in ensuring they do what is 'right'. [...] I want to favor you, this is the process and we must act contrary to what is right.
> Former DCE, National Democratic Congress

Of course, what this DCE is pressuring his staff to do is not "right". It is how the DCE and the bureaucrats survive in this political environment that is enforced by party chairs. In the ideal case, a bureaucrat could turn into a whistleblower, reporting illicit practices to superiors in the capital. This is not the case in Ghana. In interviews, many bureaucrats acknowledge that the central bureaucracy has been politicized.

> As internal auditor, I know it. And external auditors, they know it. With me, I cannot get my way, because my report goes to DCE.

Even if I send report to internal-audit agency, he [DCE] knows someone there—and he can call them to change it.

Internal Auditor, District G

In addition to such politicization in the central bureaucracy, politicians have another powerful weapon against a bureaucrat that disrupts the system: the political transfer. Wade (1982), studying the Indian case, describes the transfer mechanism as Indian politicians' chief weapon to ensure that bureaucrats extract funds for them. Brierley (2019) also describes a similar dynamic in Ghana, where politicians' ability to transfer bureaucrats corresponds with higher levels of corruption.

The interesting part is from [regional capital] to [redacted] [...] Considering my skills and knowledge I would be more useful at the center—it was a political decision against my personal wishes and expectations.

Planning Officer, District C

For party chairs, there is immense pressure to keep your foot soldiers satisfied. While foot soldiers can be deployed to support or destroy politicians, those same foot soldiers can also become dissatisfied with a party chair who does not meet their needs. A sufficient number of disgruntled foot soldiers can support a different party executive to challenge the incumbent chair during party leadership contests. Essentially, party chairs themselves are playing ultimatum games with their own foot soldiers: if a chair does not provide enough, the foot soldiers can retaliate by removing the chair from power. Chairs are under pressure to ensure that development projects are brought to their region from Accra and that districts continue to concoct project opportunities. In one district in my sample, a senior party official lamented that projects were built shoddily to ensure that the chair could re-award contracts in a few years' time for project rehabilitation. For a party chair, it is critical to amass contracts and wealth while in government to maintain one's position and fight off internal challengers.

I went to court after the [party leadership] election. [redacted] won by default. After regional elections it was only two weeks to the national elections. It's still a pain. There was a smear campaign. They said that someone came from [redacted], and sent [money] for me to give to party. [...] I took them to court for slander. Senior members pressured me to drop the case. They know it's not true, but they pleaded with me to withdraw.

Former [Party Redacted] Regional Chair

Putting the dilemmas faced by politicians, bureaucrats, contractors, and party chairs is, in sum, the Iron Square Theory of Political Finance, to play off a classic image in American politics (Adams 1981). Political finance in a developing country is a web of ultimatum games embedded within collective-action problems. As depicted in Figure 2.4, contractors exchange promised kickbacks for access to contracts, which they receive from politicians, bureaucrats, and party chairs. Expert bureaucrats legitimate a sham procurement process, which prevents auditing and ensures that politicians and chairs do not order their transfer. Bureaucrats receive access to contracts and funds to finance their retirements. Politicians provide income to finance a party chair's activities, and in turn the chair ensures that the politician has the electoral support of the party and its foot soldiers. The iron square binds these four players in a suboptimal web of dependencies on each other—the outcome of this web is poorly constructed projects, which ultimately harm the economic and social welfare of Ghana's citizens. The players in this iron square know that, around the world, projects are built each day to high quality and that such technology and know-how are not so far out of the reach of Ghanaian contractors. But why is there no movement towards building these projects better? Why have Ghanaian citizens not held these players to account?

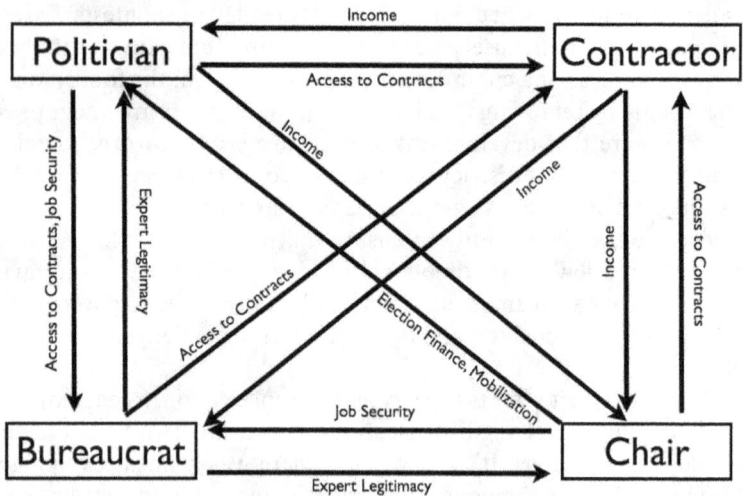

Figure 2.4 The Iron Square of Political Financing.
Source: Author.

Reshaping accountability

Bureaucrats and voters should act as safeguards to prevent or rectify the poor provision of club and public goods. Under the above system of political finance, however, both groups are compromised. In Ghana, bureaucrats are legally required to monitor the construction of projects. When those bureaucrats benefit from contract kickbacks, though, there is a conflict of interest. Rational politicians and bureaucrats will not rigorously inspect favored contractors, because those favored contractors possess a credible threat. Contractors are often allied with political-party executives, who can punish politicians and bureaucrats. Bureaucrats are acutely aware that angering contractors could impact their ability to save for retirement and meet other social obligations. As a result, bureaucrats cope by conducting only superficial inspections. Bureaucrats do not test for more technical factors such as the quality of concrete used or the installation of adequate drainage, and many projects fail within a few years.

Over time, the constraints imposed on bureaucrats by contractors and party chairs crowd out honest bureaucrats at the junior levels of the civil service. In interviews, younger bureaucrats affirmed that they joined the civil service to serve their country, but were discouraged by the corrupt actions of senior bureaucrats, who demanded their tacit complicity. Many younger bureaucrats plan to exit the public service after a few years, a situation in which only the most corruptible bureaucrats are retained.

With bureaucrats' ability to inspect effectively neutralized, contractors have incentive to construct shoddy works. If audited, bureaucrats can still plausibly claim that they followed the procurement process and inspected projects. At worst, a bureaucrat can be transferred to a different district, but their jobs will not be terminated. Shoddy contractors can easily change firm names to continue bidding on other works. Neither contractors nor bureaucrats bear the costs of shoddy construction, leading to a situation of moral hazard that perpetuates shoddy construction. The costs, rather, are inflicted on citizens.

Given that citizens bear the costs of shoddy construction, why do they not take action to rectify shoddy construction? As one MP explained,

> Why do we allow it? In Ghana, we have a culture of silence. We're not informed enough where elections are based on policy—here it's popularity and cash.[6]
>
> Member of Parliament, New Patriotic Party

Even traditional chiefs, well respected by the people, rarely criticize politicians and bureaucrats for shoddy public goods. Ensminger (2017) notes that citizens are reluctant to critique an arid-lands project in Kenya for fear of losing future projects. For Ghanaian chiefs, there is indeed fear that criticizing politicians and contractors today might result in few or no projects delivered to his village in the future. It is better to have a half-built school than no school at all.

> Yes, there is shoddy work. The District Assembly awards, but they do not involve the chiefs. Or the contract may be awarded by the region or by Accra. You cannot just tell a contractor that he is doing a bad job. He will report you to the DCE and you will get insulted. [...] On the outside, we chiefs have to welcome all contractors and pledge our support. It is our duty to ensure that all people in our villages are happy and well cared for. But on the inside we are weeping.
>
> Chief, Savannah Zone

Under a standard political-accountability model (Humphreys & Bates 2005), citizens are principals and governments are the agents that (imperfectly) serve them. Governments choose a mix of public and private goods to bestow on citizens in exchange for citizens maintaining them in power; optimally, governments will allocate the minimal amount of public goods and distributive benefits to ensure reelection, while maximizing the benefits of office-holding. In Ghana, politicians affirm that the allocation of distributive benefits to constituents is a central, exhausting feature of their job. Politicians and bureaucrats extract funds from public-goods procurement to finance the distributive benefits requested by citizens. As many citizens live near the subsistence margin, these private benefits—often hospital fees, money to buy food, or tuition payments for children—are necessary to survive, outweighing their valuation of public goods. Receipt of these distributive benefits silences citizens (Finan & Schechter 2012; Leight et al. 2019) who might otherwise eject politicians and bureaucrats for extracting funds from procurement. That is, citizens might be well aware that the club and public goods they are receiving are shoddy, but because politicians and bureaucrats have helped them survive, they will not hold them to account and risk losing those sources of assistance.

Humphreys and Bates (2005) posit that as elections become more competitive, governments must provide a greater level of public goods to remain in office. However, it is not clear whether, under increasingly competitive elections, governments will provide a greater quantity, greater quality, or both, of public goods. If distributive benefits silence citizens but allow governments to remain in office, then it is possible that governments will provide a greater quantity of public goods, but at lower quality, to finance those distributive benefits.

Conclusion

The political ecosystem is complex and interrelated. Similar to an actual ecosystem, behaviors are connected and intertwined: water that is polluted but sustains one part of the ecosystem carries that pollution to other parts of the ecosystem. In the Iron Square Theory of Political Financing, political players are entwined in costly ultimatum games with each other—and they are cemented in these games by collective-action problems that discourage individuals from changing the system. For these individuals, drinking and perpetuating polluted water is better than not drinking at all. Contractors promise kickbacks to politicians, bureaucrats, and party chairs, in exchange for the assurance that they will win contracts. Politicians use their kickbacks to finance political campaigns, citizen requests, and electoral support from party chairs. Bureaucrats allocate income from kickbacks to save for retirement and ultimately build a house. Party chairs use kickbacks to finance party foot soldiers, ensure that preferred candidates win, and maintain their own position in the party leadership. This ecosystem is legitimated by bureaucrats, whose expert approval deflects auditors.

However, the model as described above is a snapshot in time: it applies to a single governmental administration. Ghana has had many changes in party government, yet such a political-financing system persists. How does such a system persist, even when a newly elected party has been out of government—and presumably away from procurement funding—for many years? Where does that party get campaign funds? If citizens vote out an incumbent government for underperforming—*a la* the political-accountability model— then why are incoming governments not better performers? In the next chapter, I demonstrate that there are social expectations which bind the iron square of political financing and allow it to persist across governments. Beneath the political ecosystem lies a molten layer of social expectations that slowly, but deeply, moves the entire ecosystem.

Notes

1 Funds are dispersed through the DACF according to a formula. See also Banful (2008).
2 In interviews, numerous contractors complained about districts refusing to give reasons for rejecting their bids.
3 Author interview with MP, District E, April 2014.
4 However, it is not always the case that a district's politicians and bureaucrats make the first move and advertise projects. Many district officers reported that they often faced pressure from contractors and party executives to rush the advertising process so that those contractors and executives could get their funds earlier. See Ensminger (2017) for a description of similar behavior on an arid-lands development project in Kenya.
5 In the ultimatum game from game theory, there is a pool of money and, for example, two players. The first player chooses to divide the pool of money and offers a share to the second player. The second player can accept the division of money, and both players receive their shares, as divided by the first player; however, if the second player rejects the share offered—perhaps if she deems it an unfair division—then neither player receives any money.
6 The importance of personal popularity and cash to voters resembles the machine politics of the US in the early 20th century.

References

Adams, Gordon. 1981. *The Politics of Defense Contracting: The Iron Triangle.* New Brunswick, NJ: Transaction Publishers.

Apter, David. 1955. *Ghana in Transition.* Princeton, NJ: Princeton University Press.

Asante, Kojo and George Kunnath. 2018. "The Cost of Politics in Ghana." *Westminster Foundation for Democracy.* URL: http://www.wfd.org/wp-content/uploads/2018/04/Cost_Of_Politics_Ghana.pdf

Banful, Afua. 2008. "Essays on the Political Economy of Public Good Provision in Developing Countries." PhD Dissertation, Harvard University.

Bob-Milliar, George. 2012. "Political-Party Activism in Ghana: Factors Influencing the Decision of the Politically Active to Join a Political Party." *Democratization*, 19(4): 668–689.

Brierley, Sarah. 2019. "Unprincipled Principals: Co-Opted Bureaucrats and Corruption in Ghana." *American Journal of Political Science*, Forthcoming. URL: https://www.sarahbrierley.com/research.html

David-Barrett, Elizabeth and Mihaly Fazekas. 2019. "Grand Corruption and Government Change: An Analysis of Partisan Favoritism in Public Procurement." *European Journal on Criminal Policy and Research*, 25: 1–20.

District Assemblies Common Fund. 2012. "DACF Quarterly Press Releases." URL: http://commonfund.gov.gh/index.php?option=com_content&view=article&id=301&Itemid=398

Ensminger, Jean. 2017. "Corruption in Community Driven Development: A Kenyan Case Study with Insights from Indonesia." Chr. Michelsen Institute, U4 Issue 2017:9.

Finan, Frederico and Laura Schechter. 2012. "Vote-Buying and Reciprocity." *Econometrica*, 80(2): 863–881.

Fordjuor, Listowel Kwadwo. 2014. "Each MP Owes GHC 300.000—Majority Leader." URL: http://www.myjoyonline.com/politics/2014/january-19th/each-mp-owes-ghc300000-majority-leader.php

Hodgkin, Thomas. 1961. *African Political Parties*. Baltimore, MD: Penguin Books.

Humphreys, Macartan and Robert Bates. 2005. "Political Institutions and Economic Policies: Lessons from Africa." *British Journal of Political Science*, 35(3): 403–428.

Leight, Jessica, Dana Foarta, Rohini Pande, and Laura Ralston. 2019. "Value for Money? Vote-Buying and Politician Accountability." Working Paper.

Lindberg, Staffan. 2010. "What Accountability Pressures Do MPs in Africa Face and How Do They Respond? Evidence from Ghana." *Journal of Modern African Studies*, 48(1): 117–142.

Ninsin, Kwame. 2006. "Political Parties and Political Participation in Ghana." Konrad Adenauer Foundation Study. URL: https://www.kas.de/einzeltitel/-/content/political-parties-and-political-participation-in-ghana

Riordon, William. 1905. *Plunkitt of Tammany Hall: A Series of Very Plain Talks on Very Practical Politics*. New York, NY: McClure, Phillips & Co.

Schlesinger, Joseph. 1966. *Ambition and Politics: Political Careers in the United States*. Chicago, IL: Rand McNally.

Scott, James. 1969. "Corruption, Machine Politics, and Political Change." *American Political Science Review*, 63(4): 1142–1158.

The Chronicle. 2014. "MMDAs Fail to Access DDF." URL: https://www.ghanaweb.com/GhanaHomePage/NewsArchive/MMDAs-fail-to-access-DDF-337165#

Weber, Max. 1946. *From Max Weber: Essays in Sociology*. Gerth, Hans and C. Wright Mills, eds. New York, NY: Oxford University Press.

Whiteley, Paul and Patrick Seyd. 2002. *High-Intensity Participation, the Dynamics of Party Activism in Britain*. Ann Arbor: University of Michigan Press.

3 Diversification, kinship, and failed public goods

Contractors in Ghana rarely win projects without connections to the political party in power. While Ghana has passed comprehensive procurement regulations and bureaucrats are well trained, these regulations are routinely ignored. Political-party chairs wield significant influence in distributing contracts, and chairs ensure that politicians award contracts according to their wishes. To become a favored contractor, however, the contractor must credibly signal his or her loyalty to politicians and party chairs. Party chairs can ensure that political candidates win elections or are appointed to coveted offices. Chairs rally activists—known as "foot soldiers"—to increase turnout during campaigns, and these foot soldiers subsequently impose financial and social demands upon party chairs (Bob-Milliar 2012). For chairs, it is critical to amass funds to ensure electoral victory and satisfy the foot soldiers—or else they risk losing their own positions. Chairs amass much of this funding through the public-procurement process.

However, political finance based on government contracts is a risky endeavor, particularly when there are party changes in government. A party can be out of power for four years, eight years, and even longer, while the party in power strengthens itself. Contractors loyal to opposition politicians will not win government contracts, which means they may go out of business. Political aspirants of the opposition also cannot benefit from these contracts. How do players cope with the risk of being out of power? How do opposition parties find the funds to successfully challenge an incumbent government?

In addition, the riskiness of government contracting in Ghana affects the quality of the work that is performed. If a contractor needs to use funds to signal loyalty to chairs, politicians, and bureaucrats (i.e., pay kickbacks), then that contractor will have less money with which to complete the work. Tying contracts to political loyalty and financing reduces the quality of work that contractors can perform.

As a result, the public suffers. There are countless stories in Ghanaian media outlets about schools that are only partially built or district-assembly buildings that immediately spring leaky roofs. The risks and hidden costs that contractors must face lower the quality of public goods—which ultimately lowers citizens' trust that the government can provide public goods.

In this chapter, I focus on small-scale contractors who operate at the local levels, rather than large international firms which typically bid on much larger projects, such as highways and airports. While local contractors in Ghana are motivated by profits, most live close to the subsistence margin, meaning that they are likely to prefer minimizing income volatility instead of maximizing income (Scott 1976). Though agriculture is the largest source of employment for Ghanaians, many are exiting agriculture to start construction firms. Any entrepreneurial Ghanaian can start a construction business, especially because there is little enforcement of the requirements to register as a qualified contractor. Despite private demand for contractors increasing in urban areas, the Government of Ghana remains the largest purchaser of contractor services.

Firms and kinship

There are few barriers to entry in Ghana's construction industry. While the Ministry for Water Resources, Works, and Housing mandates that contractors meet education and technical requirements, in reality, these criteria are rarely enforced, reducing the average expertise and capacity of contractors. Though most rural Ghanaians have historically been employed in small-scale agriculture, many have realized poor returns and are exiting agriculture to start their own construction firms. Being a contractor by no means guarantees a stable income, but many are seduced by the industry because there can be occasional windfalls—such as when a local politician or chair rises to a higher office.

> Simple thing, easiest thing, to do is to decide to become a contractor. He knows a way. He knows true politics. If he knows the party in power, he may get something to do.
>
> Contractor, District C

Being a successful contractor can also bring one prestige as well as financial opportunities to engage in other businesses. With each successful contract brought in, contractors can serve as informal bankers for their communities. In rural Ghana, most citizens lack access to formal banking (CGAP 2011). Lacking access to banks, aspiring entrepreneurs have few options for raising capital to start a business. Contractors can access lucrative sums through government projects, and many report that they provide capital for rural entrepreneurs to start businesses. Behind many of the small businesses in Ghana—whether a tailors' shop, convenience store, or restaurant—there is likely a connection to a contractor who provided some funds and building materials.

With its potential for lucrative profits, the contractors' market in Ghana is governed by political favor, and political favor is inherently uncertain. While Ghana has enacted public-procurement regulations (Act 663), such regulations are often flouted or otherwise ignored. Projects are awarded to contractors loyal to the political actors in power, and, in exchange, winning contractors deliver kickbacks to support political campaigns. Many contractors are themselves party foot soldiers. However, it is possible for the party to lose the next election, depriving the loyal contractor of her patron and income source. Some of these contractors can change firm names and decide to support the other party or candidate, though there are certainly risks to doing that frequently. For many contractors, being directly involved in politics is too risky and they stay out to avoid harming their personal reputations.

To survive, Ghanaian contractors rely on two safety nets: income diversification and kinship networks. On the first safety net, contractors in Ghana operate side businesses to bolster income streams when contracts and subcontracts are not forthcoming. Such income streams can dry up if a contractor is known to support a party that is not in power. Income streams can also dry up for government-supporting contractors if there are not enough projects to go around or if district-assembly funding is delayed. Many contractors sell or rent construction materials on the side, such as cement, iron rods, mixers, and dump trucks. These are attractive options since, even if contracts are only awarded to a small group of construction businesses, that group still needs materials or equipment. In addition to construction materials and equipment, many contractors also offer consulting and engineering services on the side.

However, contractors do not limit themselves to just side businesses related to the construction industry. Many contractors also operate accommodations, restaurants, bars, gas stations, transportation services, and myriad other types of small businesses—anything to have a somewhat stable revenue stream. I frequently interviewed contractors in my sample at such side businesses, and several pointed out other side businesses around town owned by themselves or other contractors. Construction can indeed be a gateway for accessing the capital to operate small businesses—though those small businesses also form an income safety net for these contractors.

Though contractors can operate numerous side businesses to cushion themselves against income shocks, they still have to be careful about how such businesses are advertised. In many areas of the country, certain businesses are seen as owned by an "NDC man" or an "NPP man". Politicians have been known to avoid staying at certain accommodations or eating at certain restaurants to avoid the appearance of patronizing establishments that support—and presumably finance—the opposition. To protect against partisan perceptions, many contractors placed other family members as heads of these side companies. For contractors that do not wish to explicitly support a party or whose preferred party is in the opposition, side businesses offer viable options for survival.

> If the projects are not coming in, you sit down and do nothing. That is why I have small businesses! That's so I can survive whether rain or shine.
>
> Contractor, District C

It is important to note that contractors in Ghana are representative of other Ghanaians: they are looking to survive financially and, hopefully, prosper. While contractors do go to great lengths to diversify their incomes and downplay partisan connections that their side businesses may have, all contractors know that their brother and sister contractors are making similar decisions. In a way, contractors know that they are all in this together. As such, I found that in my sample many contractors did rely on each other's various businesses for financial support, whether for construction projects or not.

With respect to familial relationships, kinship norms are central to the functioning of Ghanaian society. These norms deeply move and shape all parts of the political ecosystem, regardless of party affiliation. Contrary to language that might be seen during political debates on television, many of my politician and party-chair respondents referred to each other as brothers and sisters, even if they were referring to members of different parties and ethnic groups. Many respondents used the language of "taking care" of their constituents as if they were family members.

Following Winick (1956) and La Ferrara (2008), I define "kin group" to denote persons that comprise "socially recognized relationships based on supposed as well as actual genealogical ties". What is key in this definition is that kin-group members do not have to be biologically related.

In common parlance, a kinship group may be thought of as one's "extended family". Insurance provided by one's kin group is important in societies facing unpredictable shocks (Scott 1976; La Ferrara 2008). During periods of economic hardship, a struggling household can turn to a more successful household for assistance. Scott (1976), studying Vietnam, reaffirms the reciprocity of peasant relations: "It is also evident that as soon as a peasant leans on his kin or his patron rather than on his own resources, he gives them a reciprocal claim to his own labor and resources". When the successful household struggles, they can then turn to the other household for assistance, who are obliged to help.

Breaking one's kinship obligations to help others will incur significant social sanctioning, and Hoff and Sen (2005) note that many kin groups erect exit barriers to prevent members from shirking their obligations. Such exit barriers enforce kinship norms and reciprocity. For instance, many respondents indicated that Ghana does not have a "culture" of criticizing politicians, bureaucrats, contractors, and party chairs for executing poor public works. Those guilty of executing poor public works are frequently seen to "walk free". Despite the "open secret" of corruption and poor project delivery, why are Ghanaian citizens so hesitant to criticize those responsible? Even many chiefs, the most prominent citizens at the village level, are apprehensive about criticizing politicians. I posit that such hesitancy to criticize is related to kinship norms, norms that help to preserve social harmony and reduce uncertainties. That politician or bureaucrat or contractor who has performed their duties poorly today may have helped you in the past, or she may help you again in the future. But choosing to criticize that person now may harm your social standing and terminate any future opportunities for support. For citizens who are just trying to survive, losing such future support could be unbearable.

In Ghana, kinship networks intersect with formal political rules to perpetuate the iron square of political financing, even with party changes in government. The President of Ghana appoints all Regional Ministers and District Chief Executives (DCEs), even in areas where the ruling party is weak, which ensures that both major parties are present throughout the country, rather than being localized to stronghold areas. There will always be National Democratic Congress (NDC)- and New Patriotic Party (NPP)-affiliated contractors in each district, ready to be awarded a government's projects when their party is in power. However, in many regions, there can be overwhelming numbers of NDC contractors and party supporters and very few NPP contractors and supporters, and vice versa. Because the executive appoints all DCEs and Regional Ministers, who have access to contracts, what happens when the NDC is locally in power in an NPP-majority area or when the NPP is in power in an NDC-majority area?

While the two major parties appear to be enemies in the media, in reality, kinship binds the parties together at the local level and relations can be cordial and mutually beneficial.[1] For contractors in districts across Ghana, such kinship relations across party lines can be the key to survival when one's party is out of power. Contractors in each district are often related to each other by family ties or other associations. Because of reciprocity norms, contractors, regardless of political affiliation, frequently—but not always—assist each other. For instance, contractors rarely own all the equipment needed to complete a project, and it is common for fellow contractors to lend dump trucks, cement mixers, and other equipment. More importantly, when a contractor receives a government project, she can subcontract portions, such as plumbing or electricals, to opposition contractors, as detailed in Figure 3.1. This subcontracting is especially the case if the original general contractor lacks the equipment, staff, or expertise to complete the entire project herself. Those opposition contractors then have funds to survive while their party is out of power—and they

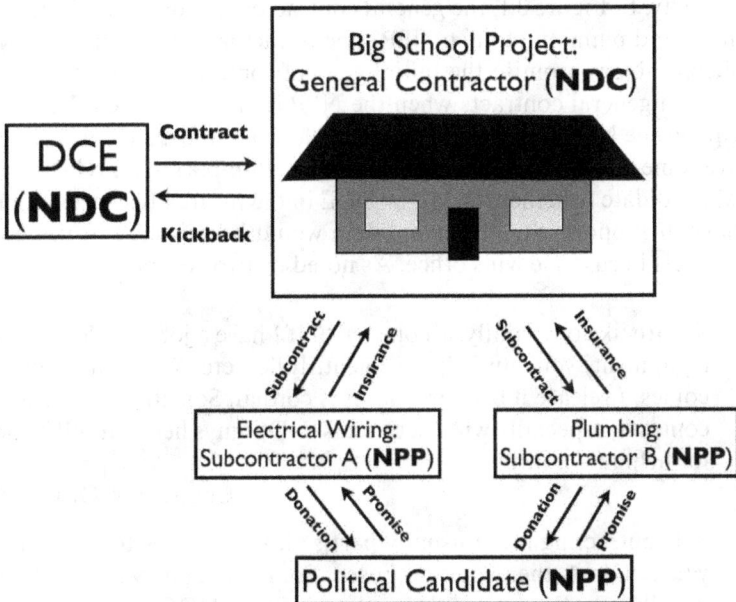

Figure 3.1 Subcontracting Across Party Lines.
Source: Author.

can also use a portion of those subcontracted funds to support their own party's political candidates, who would promise future contracts. Should the opposition come to power, those subcontractors would then be obliged to help the first contractor. As such, the initial general contractor has insurance against future income shocks.

In Figure 3.1, the NDC DCE has "awarded" a big school contract to a loyal NDC general contractor. In line with the iron square, that contractor has provided a kickback to the DCE, bolstering the DCE's political finances. While local school projects across Ghana are relatively uniform (e.g., three-classroom blocks, six-classroom blocks, and teacher bungalows), most do have multiple components, such as plumbing, electricals, car parks (covered or uncovered), sports fields, and kitchens.[2] If the general contractor has the equipment and expertise to build these components, then she can.

However, in my interviews with contractors, many lacked the ability to complete the full construction project. As such, they turned to their brother and sister contractors for assistance. Sometimes these subcontractors were of the same party as the general contractor, but many contractors reported to me that they subcontracted to (or received subcontracts from) kin members affiliated with the other political party. In Figure 3.1, the general contractor subcontracts electrical wiring and plumbing to two NPP subcontractors. In exchange, those subcontractors promise the initial general contractor "insurance"; if they win general contracts when the NPP is in charge, then they will help out the NDC general contractor.[3] Now that these subcontractors have some money, they can provide financial support to an NPP political candidate (whether for MP or DCE in the future). Because of that financial support, the NPP candidate would be expected to provide contracts in case she wins office. As noted by two contractors,

> We are like one family, all one tribe. If I have a job and don't have equipment, you can help—cement, roller, etc. When my cement comes, I release it back to you. It is cordial. Sometimes we'll subcontract, especially with electricals. NDC guys help out NPP now for help in the future.
>
> Contractor, District C

> Subcontracting is not usually partisan. If you come to mind, and you can do it, then you are chosen. Sometimes party matters, but usually not. We are brothers. If an NPP or NDC man does us a favor, we will return it. It happens.
>
> Contractor, District A

However, while subcontracting (both to contractors loyal to the opposition and those that were not) was cited by many contractors as a common phenomenon, some contractors in my sample reported that they rarely received subcontracts.

> Some are friendly. With subcontracting, Ghana is like this: I have had only one subcontract. Most of them are greedy, and they won't give it to you. It is very difficult to get subcontracts here—I've only seen one. Even when lamenting to my friends.
>
> Contractor, District H

While kinship norms are helpful to receiving subcontracts, they may not be an ironclad guarantee. Thus, it is important to also have side businesses to maintain some flow of revenue.

From the formal, legal standpoint, the ability to subcontract to firms within one's kin group is beneficial. Such subcontracting allows a firm to claim that it has access to all necessary equipment should an auditor inquire (which is rare), as the subcontractee firm may have "access" to equipment. Officially, most firms do not *own* all the capital equipment they need, such as cement mixers or dump trucks, but, because of kinship relations, these firms can *access* the equipment owned by their brothers and sisters. Similarly, individual firms rarely have all the expertise they need to complete a project. Such experts would include engineers, architects, quantity surveyors, accountants, and various other skilled jobs. Many of the firm owners I interviewed were trained in one of these fields—but they rarely had permanent staff who were trained in the other fields. In a way, many local projects in Ghana are constructed by committees bound by kinship.

Kinship reciprocity is important for contractors because of how close many of them are to subsistence or the threshold for survival. Focusing on Vietnamese peasant life, Scott (1976) delineates the "subsistence ethic": being close to subsistence changes how an agent acts, resulting in deviations from rational economic theory. Such agents adopt a "safety first" strategy towards income (Scott 1976). That is, peasants will be risk averse and forgo maximizing profits to establish a minimum, stable income level that prevents starvation. To establish a minimum income above subsistence, contractors in Ghana spread their risk and overall income across multiple sources. Bates (2001) describes the Kikuyu's methods for minimizing risk by engaging in agricultural activities in diverse climactic zones and investing in kin members who have migrated to urban centers. Scott (1976) writes that "risk dispersal has also been observed among poor ex-peasants who may respond to the risk of unemployment by pursuing several minor occupations to minimize the danger of ever being entirely out of work".

While subcontracts and side businesses stabilize contractors' incomes above the subsistence margin, ultimately such activities discourage investment in the firm. During periods in which a construction firm's outputs are in demand (e.g., they receive a contract from the DCE), the successful firm's owner is obliged to subcontract because she lacks capital equipment or has kinship obligations to fulfill, which diminishes the profit she would receive as well as the amount she could use to invest. The cost of breaking one's kinship obligations outweighs the benefit of investing in one's firm. A person that is blacklisted by one's kin group for not honoring her obligations may be forced to relocate and integrate into an unfamiliar location, which inflicts significant costs. Side businesses can distract an owner from her core construction firm, reducing her ability and financial resources to upgrade skills and equipment.

Firms, investment, and construction quality

Under conditions of demand uncertainty, firms under-invest in themselves rather than risk idling excess capital (Pindyck 1988; Bates 2000; Pattillo 2000). Pindyck (1988) illuminates this concept for marginal investments by incorporating McDonald and Siegel's (1986) option value of waiting to invest. When deciding to invest, a firm's owner considers not just the cost of implementing the investment and its expected returns: she must also consider the cost of giving up the option to invest at a future time, when conditions or other information might be more favorable. For firm owners, it is the irreversibility of investments that induces them to hold less capacity in case demand drops; once a steel factory is built, its cost is sunk, and diminished demand for steel will reduce the value of that plant (Pindyck 1988). In terms of construction, a firm owner can decide to purchase a dump truck or a cement mixer today— or it might be more profitable in the long run to purchase that equipment in the future, in case the firm is more likely to receive contracts then.

Construction firms in Ghana align well with Pindyck's (1988) framework. There is significant uncertainty in terms of demand for a contractor's services, and much of that demand depends on political favor. Contractors do not know when a district might be tendering for new projects, and they do not know for certain whether politicians or bureaucrats will give them projects. As a result, many Ghanaian firms under-invest in themselves due to the risk of having to finance and maintain idle construction equipment. Contractors whose party is out of power and who must rely on subcontracts are particularly affected by income shocks, and so would be very unlikely to invest in their firms. Further, purchasing construction equipment is an uncertain endeavor, and such equipment is subject to the "market for lemons" (Akerlof 1970). Though equipment may be bought new, their resale value drops immediately as future buyers are imperfectly able to differentiate between high- and low-quality used construction machinery. For contractors, there is little resale value in used construction equipment, which heightens the risk of buying capital for one's firm. Should a contractor choose to borrow and pay for capital equipment in installments, she might not receive contract income necessary to make payments. When a foot soldier or other contractor receives a contract, she will rely on subcontractors with complementary pieces of equipment to complete the project. Equipment that is shared and spread across multiple contractors, however, can delay construction, especially if the equipment is shared across geographically disparate projects. Additionally, due to principal-agent problems, such equipment may deteriorate faster if those who borrow it are not well observed by the owner of the equipment.

I depart from Pindyck's (1988) framework, however, in its discussion of the option value of waiting. As mentioned above, many Ghanaian citizens enter Ghana's construction industry due to its low barriers to entry, its relative mobility (and risk dispersal), and its potential for lucrative gains. These citizens live close to the subsistence margin and cannot wait long for the next contract to arrive. There is little worth to the option value of waiting to invest as waiting would jeopardize one's survival. Ghanaian contractors are, thus, faced with a risky dilemma: they are averse to capital investment due to the uncertainty of political favor-based contracting, but they have little patience to invest in future time periods due to their proximity to the subsistence margin.

With little incentive to invest in one's firm, whether in the present or future, construction quality suffers. Many contractors reported to me that they and their colleagues would use fewer bags of cement on a project when they knew they were running short of funds (e.g., through bribes or because of subcontracts). Without new or well-maintained cement mixers, Ghanaian contractors cannot create quality cement to be used in buildings; such shoddy quality will become noticeable within a few months or years. In Ghana, there is little reward for a contractor who builds quality work. Such demonstrations of long-term quality do not necessarily attract more business in the same way that they would in other markets. Rather, chairs and politicians receive kickbacks from favored contractors to finance vote-buying and other political activities in the short term, activities which suppress accountability measures that voters might otherwise exercise (Kitschelt 2000; Finan & Schechter 2012; Leight et al. 2019). Without voters to protest shoddy construction, contractors who devote funds and efforts to quality construction only harm themselves.

Along with shoddily constructed projects, many projects simply never get finished. Williams (2017), drawing from a database of 14,000 local-development projects across Ghana, finds that approximately one-third of local-development projects that are started are never completed. Similar to responses from many of the contractors in my sample, Williams (2017) finds that many contractors face uncertainty in receiving payments for their work or are ultimately underpaid. Williams (2017) explains projects fail to be completed because of a dynamically inconsistent collective-choice problem amongst local political actors. That is, in a district, multiple actors must bargain over how a limited number of projects will be distributed and implemented; over time, because these coalitions of actors can be unstable, collective priorities may shift to different projects. As a result, since it can take months for projects to be completed, started projects are stopped mid-construction as the local government decides to build the next set of projects. Williams (2017) further argues that observed project non-completion is likely not driven by corruption or clientelism.

While Williams's (2017) finding that sizeable numbers of local-development projects in Ghana are left incomplete should not be surprising to observers of the country, it is difficult to deny the role that corruption and clientelism play in shaping how contracts are allocated and how contractors behave towards these projects. It is true that many local governments in Ghana face unstable collective priorities; however, the iron square suggests that politicians, bureaucrats, contractors, and party chairs have an incentive to award more projects, even if existing projects are not complete, so that they can access more rent-seeking opportunities—rents that can be converted to private goods to suppress voters' agitations for project completion. As a result, local governments' dynamically inconsistent priorities are related to the corrupted logics that shape how politicians, bureaucrats, contractors, and party leaders behave. Many local governments bring in additional projects, knowing that started projects may not be completed. As noted by one bureaucrat,

> Another thing, the politicians, against all technical advice, award too many projects! We can't pay! They say, 'In my time, people need to know I am working!' They know we don't have the funds to pay.
> Assistant Planning Officer, District J

Contractors frequently reported being underpaid or paid late for the contracts that they receive. However, many contractors indicated that they would not wait for payment before constructing works—such payments from the district or central government could take up to two years to arrive. As such, contractors would construct as much of a project as quickly as possible, and frequently with fewer materials than required given bribes that are paid along the way. If the contractor has borrowed staff or materials, then it is likely that he only has a fixed amount of time in which he can use such staff and materials. Contractors realize that waiting to purchase materials, knowing that you have a contract in hand, is risky because inflation could raise the cost of those materials; however, there is rarely provision in the contracts to insure a contractor against price increases.

Political and demand uncertainties raise challenges for contractors who prefer to construct quality works and not engage in political favoritism. There is a high risk that losing political favoritism or not having your party in power will lead to a firm not receiving contracts for an extended period of time. Some firms misrepresent the quality of their goods in the market, but are able to curry political favor, which drives out legitimate firms. Many quality contractors in Ghana have already exited the construction market, taking their expertise with them. The quality firms that remain must rely on side businesses and subcontracts to survive during leaner times; however, these subcontracts may not be sufficient to construct quality works. Ultimately, because of the bribes that are paid, lack of firm investment, and kinship pressures to subcontract for future insurance, the quality of construction of Ghana's local-development projects suffers. Many projects are started but are left incomplete—and unfortunately, because of kinship norms, those who are responsible for shoddy, incomplete work are not held to account.

Firm mergers?

Though many construction firms already take advantage of subcontracting to share their equipment with other firms, especially for more complex projects, few Ghanaian firms merge. Most construction firms in Ghana are small, family-run businesses. These firms, on their own, can only build small projects, such as elementary schools, market stalls, and public latrines—conditional on having political connections. However, despite kinship connections, there is little interest amongst firm owners to merge their firms. This is a puzzle since one would expect larger firms to be able to compete more effectively for contracts.

> It's difficult because of our legal system. People don't understand business law. Company is seen as a family thing. Construction companies don't float shares or have shareholders. Here it's my business, when I die, it goes to my kids. We haven't gotten to that stage.
>
> Contractor, District K

Inheritance traditions in Ghana may discourage firms from merging. The Akan, Ghana's predominant ethnic group, practices matrilineal inheritance. For a man, property is not passed to his own son upon his death, but rather his sister's son (La Ferrara 2007). While alive, there are few limits to asset transfers from parents to their children. Businesses can be shared with one's children, and this arrangement allows parents, while alive, to transfer assets directly to their children in exchange for future elder care (La Ferrara 2007). Keeping a business small, but above the subsistence margin, ensures that the family maintains a stable income stream that is theirs alone. Such stability is critical. It is simply too risky for individual contractors to share their small business outside of the immediate family. For many of these contractors, keeping their business inside the family ensures that children can inherit a source of income and provide care to elder family members.

However, there are other options for firms to expand their capacity. For instance, firms can form cooperatives or associations to join resources and be more competitive. In Ghana, many farmers have experience forming agricultural cooperatives, such as in the cocoa sector (Hiscox, Hainmueller, & Tampe 2011). These cooperatives can form around key practices, such as fair trade, organic methods, or single-source farming. With their capital and expertise pooled in a cooperative, construction firms could access loans to acquire more capital equipment and invest in themselves. Such construction cooperatives can also apply for licenses that would allow them to compete for larger government projects, which are typically built by only the largest firms or foreign firms.

> I'm appointed [as an officer of the local contractors' association]. My role is to write to all contractors in region. The chair [of the association] realizes that most contractors die poor. We want to acquire license so we can compete with foreign companies. This is one way to combat against 10 percent and politicians. We have

over 200 members, and, as far as active members, we have about 150. Some are doing small business. We have some members with active work—about 60—but others are still owed by the Government of Ghana.

Contractor, District H

This particular contractor association is ambitious and is using the size of its membership to apply for a license to be a larger-scale contractor. In a few other regions of my sample, contractors mentioned that they were members of an association. However, managing a cooperative is by no means straightforward. With so many members, how will revenues be divided? How will equipment be shared and maintained? Such a cooperative needs clear rules and enforcement to ensure its stability. Cooperatives require trust and continued commitment from their members. Without such norms, disgruntled members could defect from the cooperative or compete against it, lowering chances of winning a contract. Nonetheless, even if the cooperative solves those dilemmas and receives a license, it is not clear that they will win contracts without political contacts, without their "10 percent".

Conclusion

Contractors have a variety of strategies for surviving when their party is out of power or when they are otherwise out of political favor. Many run side businesses, such as providing materials or services to contractors who are able to receive contracts. Outside of side businesses, kinship reciprocity allows a contractor to survive when political actors do not favor her. Contractors can receive subcontracts from members of their kin group so that they can have some income to survive. However, when times are favorable, reciprocity norms can reduce a contractor's revenues as she must assist other contractors instead of investing to improve her own firm. Ultimately, construction firms in Ghana are unable to upgrade their capital equipment, and they cannot construct larger or more complex works. Over time, quality contractors exit the industry and are replaced by opportunistic foot soldiers who lack the expertise to construct quality works. Unless steps are taken to reduce contractors' uncertainty and improve their capacity, Ghana's infrastructure is unlikely to improve.

It is difficult to recommend an appropriate course of action for donors. On the one hand, donors should not construct local development projects with foreign firms—such firms could further drive out the local construction expertise that is already in short supply. On the other hand, Ghanaian contractors are caught in a trap. While each firm would like to make stable revenues and construct more complex, quality projects, they are embedded in a system where they must construct with fewer funds. Some firms are attempting to form cooperatives, but even those endeavors face their own management and coordination challenges—not to mention that they would likely still need political favor to win contracts.

Despite these difficulties and the uncertainty of revenue streams, it is amazing that qualified contractors still stay in the industry. Contractors could exit to other industries, such as farming or transportation, but many of my respondents treated construction as a labor of love.

> The beauty of it—when you hand over, especially a village classroom block, and see kids run into the classroom, you feel so fine. I've not been paid, but that little boy is going to wake up and be in school tomorrow. That keeps me in the business.
>
> Contractor, District K

Countless other contractors described with pride the various public toilets, market stalls, school blocks, and other local infrastructure projects that they had handed off to the public. Of course, I am sure many of these contractors knew that those projects were not constructed to the highest quality and that they had not used the appropriate number of bags of cement. Many of those contractors knew that they had paid their illegal 10% (or 20%–30%) to secure a contract—and that they would still struggle to even survive. Likely most of those contractors ended those projects, waited extensive periods of time for full payment from the government, and still walked away with less money than they expected. Nonetheless, there are still qualified contractors left in the industry from whom construction is more than just work—it is a public service. But it is not clear how much longer those contractors can hold out.

As contractors increasingly find themselves trapped in these dilemmas with uncertain revenue streams, the public starts to realize that it is seeing the same bad outcome over and over again—specifically, shoddy construction. Shoddy construction, by its very physical, visible nature, erodes public confidence in government. Shoddy construction means market stalls that barely protect one's goods or schools that are not conducive to learning or clinics that lack sanitary conditions. Citizens that suffer these poor club and public goods start asking their politicians for private favors: money to send their children to a different school or money to send a sick family member to a private clinic in a different town. But politicians, to help their constituents, must get that money from somewhere. The irony is that citizens' demands for private goods from politicians, bureaucrats, contractors, and parties start to literally erode the club and public goods that governments are expected to provide. The vicious cycle persists.

Kinship obligations underlie the political ecosystem of the iron square. These obligations are the molten layer of expectations that slowly, but surely, moves the groundwork of the political ecosystem; such behavioral norms are deeply rooted in a country. Even if there is a disruption in the political ecosystem, where one party loses power and another prevails, kinship obligations—and the threat of social ostracism for not meeting those obligations—weigh on each player in the iron square, hindering their ability to provide quality public goods or protest against the system. As such, the iron square persists, despite the promises of a new government for reform—the foot soldiers and loyal contractors of that new government must still rely on reciprocal obligations to insure themselves against future losses. The funds that arise from this system of political finance are used to buy votes, which suppresses the public's ability to hold governments and contractors to account. Given these constraints, what would it take for players within the iron square to successfully change the system? What can those on the outside do?

Notes

1 That is not to say that there are never flare-ups between the parties in the local areas. However, most of the time, in most places, party members do get along with each other despite party differences.
2 These construction projects typically do not include the materials that would go inside the school, such as desks, chalkboards, and classroom supplies. Those materials would undergo their own procurement process—and be subject to yet more potential procurement corruption.
3 It is important to note here that the general contractor has an incentive to withhold some money from the subcontract as a "fee" for providing this service to the subcontractor. Thus, it is likely that the subcontractor will have less funding with which to construct their portion of the project.

References

Akerlof, George. 1970. "The Market for 'Lemons': Quality Uncertainty and the Market Mechanism." *Quarterly Journal of Economics*, 84(3), 488–500.
Bates, Robert. 2000. "So What Have We Learned?" In Paul Collier and catherine Pattillo (eds.), *Investment and Risk in Africa*, pp. 365–372. New York, NY: St. Martin's Press.

Bates, Robert. 2001. *Prosperity and Violence: The Political Economy of Development.* New York, NY: W.W. Norton.

Bob-Milliar, George. 2012. "Political-Party Activism in Ghana: Factors Influencing the Decision of the Politically Active to Join a Political Party." *Democratization*, 19(4): 668–689.

Consultative Group to Assist the Poorest (CGAP). 2011. "Technology Program Country Note: Ghana." URL: https://www.cgap.org/sites/default/files/CGAP-Technology-Program-Country-Note-Ghana-Jun-2011.pdf

Finan, Frederico and Laura Schechter. 2012. "Vote-Buying and Reciprocity." *Econometrica*, 80(2): 863–881.

Government of Ghana. 2003. *Act 663: Public Procurement Act.* URL: https://www.ppaghana.org/documents/Public%20Procurement%20Act%202003%20Act%20663.pdf

Hiscox, Michael, Jens Hainmueller, and Maja Tampe. 2011. "Sustainable Development for Cocoa Farmers in Ghana." IGC Working Paper.

Hoff, Karla and Arijit Sen. 2005. "The Kin System as a Poverty Trap?" World Bank Policy Research Working Paper 3575.

Kitschelt, Herbert. 2000. "Linkages between Citizens and Politicians in Democratic Polities." *Comparative Political Studies*, 33(6): 845–879.

La Ferrara, Eliana. 2007. "Descent Rules and Strategic Transfers: Evidence from Matrilineal Groups in Ghana." *Journal of Development Economics*, 83(2): 280–301.

La Ferrara, Eliana. 2008. "Family and Kinship Ties in Development: An Economist's Perspective." *Afrique Contemporaine*, 226: 61–84.

Leight, Jessica, Dana Foarta, Rohini Pande, and Laura Ralston. 2019. "Value for Money? Vote-Buying and Politician Accountability." Working Paper.

McDonald, Robert and Daniel Siegel. 1986. "The Value of Waiting to Invest." *Quarterly Journal of Economics*, 101(4): 707–728.

Pattillo, Catherine. 2000. "Risk, Financial Constraints, and Equipment Investment in Ghana: A Firm-Level Analysis." In Paul Collier and Catherine Pattillo, *Investment and Risk in Africa*, 96–121. New York, NY: St. Martin's Press.

Pindyck, Robert. 1988. "Irreversible Investment, Capacity Choice, and the Value of the Firm." *American Economic Review*, 78(5): 969–985.

Scott, James. 1976. *The Moral Economy of the Peasant: Rebellion and Subsistence in Southeast Asia.* New Haven, CT: Yale University Press.

Williams, Martin. 2017. "The Political Economy of Unfinished Development Projects: Corruption, Clientelism, or Collective Choice?" *American Political Science Review*, 111(4): 705–723.

Winick, Charles. 1956. *Dictionary of Anthropology.* New York, NY: Philosophical Library.

Conclusion
Towards antiheroes and Machine-Guided Development

In Ghana, political activities are financed by an iron square of politicians, bureaucrats, contractors, and political-party chairs who extract kickbacks from public procurement. Politicians and bureaucrats—often under pressure from party chairs—collude to divide projects amongst themselves so that their preferred contractors will receive projects. Contractors, in exchange for receiving projects, kick back a percentage of a project's award funds to those who have helped their firm receive a project. While many politicians, bureaucrats, contractors, and party chairs recognize the inefficiency and corruption of the iron square, they are impelled by personal and social pressures to sustain this system. Politicians need funds to win elections and satisfy constituents. Bureaucrats need funds for retirement. Contractors need funds to survive. Chairs need funds to support foot soldiers, who canvas for politicians and provide other assistance. Various combinations of these players are locked in collective-action dilemmas that stymie attempts to change the system. The players in this political ecosystem are polluting and over-extracting the water (money) that nourishes them all, ultimately hindering improvement in the provision of public goods.

The iron square binding this political ecosystem is not limited to a particular party in government. Despite regular elections, political promises to combat corruption, and party changes in government, the iron square of political financing persists. Undergirding the persistence of local procurement corruption is an intricate web of social norms, preferences for income stabilization, and reciprocity. When a contractor receives a project under this system, she faces a strong incentive to subcontract portions of that project to other contractors (including those aligned with the opposition party) so that those contractors can survive when not directly receiving contracts. In turn, such subcontracting generates an obligation: those subcontractors will help the initial contractor should her party be voted out in the next election. Those subcontractors are themselves using these funds to support potential opposition candidates. While this system of reciprocal subcontracting helps contractors to survive, it discourages firms from investing in equipment and expertise, which can lower construction quality over time.

Given the structure of this iron square and the deeply rooted incentives sustaining it, where does this leave the community of development scholars and practitioners? It is tempting to surrender and concede that the collective-action problems and reciprocity norms present insurmountable obstacles to improving local-development outcomes. It is tempting to assume that overall better global trade and economic growth will trickle down and benefit local communities. Some donors would affirm that better procurement practices or more advanced technologies would resolve corruption and poor public-goods provision. It is not clear that the problems described in this book are particular to a given level of technology. The goal of this chapter is not to describe a problem and donors' unsuccessful efforts to date, but rather to identify aspects of a given system that can be changed—with both local and outside support—and thus offer a potential way forward.

Modernization and political development

Conventional theories of modernization would suggest that economic development will improve the quality of democracy in a given country (Lipset 1960; Apter 1965). Supporters of modernization theory argue that as countries develop economically, there is less demand from citizens and voters for private goods from politicians and increased demand for "programmatic" policies, such as better healthcare, education, transportation, and so forth. To engage with how political actors might approach the tensions between providing private versus public goods, Stokes et al. (2013) present a broker-mediated model of party politics. In this model, political brokers are imperfect agents of party-leadership principals. These brokers, similar to precinct captains in US political machines or regional chairs and foot soldiers in Ghana, are the boots on the ground. They understand the needs of poor voters, and they can provide private resources (e.g., money, jobs, and contracts) to those voters in exchange for their votes supporting the party. As Stokes et al. (2013) demonstrate, these resources typically go to party supporters. Such brokers, though, skim resources for themselves, thereby imposing a cost on the party and its leaders, who might prefer to target resources at swing voters.

In Stokes et al.'s (2013) model of broker-mediated machine politics, party leaders face a challenge: they can continue to condone brokers' extraction of resources associated with vote buying, or they can dismantle these machines in favor of more programmatic methods of winning votes. Drawing from examples in the UK and US, Stokes et al. (2013) posit that party leaders will dismantle their machines once the costs of a broker-mediated machine are outweighed by the benefits of conducting programmatic campaigns. In the UK and US, industrialization changed the nature of the electorate, growing the middle class—voters who should theoretically have less need for the private goods provided by party machines. Further, advances in communication allowed party leaders to reach voters more directly, lessening the importance of brokers who directly know their voters.

With respect to modernization theory, those initial arguments were first posed over half a century ago, and there have been numerous theoretical and empirical critiques of modernization theory. For developing countries, how much longer will it take for "modernization" to improve political institutions and development outcomes? Since the early 1990s, numerous African states have undergone democratic transitions, and observers have noted that several countries have seen peaceful party changes in government. Nonetheless, as this book demonstrates, non-programmatic politics based on the exchange of private goods is still prevalent in Ghana—and the processes, such as political financing, that underline these non-programmatic exchanges undermine programmatic public goods and services. Despite further advances in communication and the rise of social media, Ghana's foot soldiers and their local knowledge are still highly relevant to politics.

Additionally, since the early 1990s, donors have supplied significant funds to aid democratization in the developing world (Carothers & de Gramont 2013). Such funds have been targeted at supporting electoral commissions, strengthening political parties, empowering journalists, amongst other activities. But while donor countries have—using their own countries as examples of "successful" democratization—supported democratization in developing countries, it is not clear that developed democracies have demonstrated how politics can be financed. In other words, developing countries have received myriad funds and technical assistance to conduct democratic processes, but there has been little assistance with respect to raising funds for campaigns in ways that do not compromise candidates and other actors. How can a developing country meet its democratic obligations, if its candidates cannot pay for their campaigns in an honest fashion? Of course, developed countries themselves have not solved issues of political finance, and in many developed countries there are numerous instances of money's negative role in politics (Lessig 2011). Thus, developing countries are at a disadvantage—they have adopted the external democratic institutions advised by donor countries but there has been little guidance on how to finance such institutions.

Alternative perspectives on modernization and development

While modernization theory predicts that economic development would improve democratic politics and the delivery of public goods and services, recent scholarship on urbanization in sub-Saharan Africa suggests otherwise. Urban populations in sub-Saharan Africa have grown significantly in recent decades, but it is not clear how such urbanization will impact political processes that have, to date, been grounded in the non-programmatic provision of private goods. In these urban areas, an African middle class is growing. To what extent is this middle class driving a shift from non-programmatic provision of private and club goods to programmatic provision of quality public goods and services?

Nathan (2019), examining the case of Accra, Ghana, finds that political processes in urban environments embrace a mix of programmatic and non-programmatic appeals. In poorer urban environments, parties and politicians continue to employ non-programmatic provision, offering private goods and "constituency service" to voters in exchange for their support for the party. Such non-programmatic provision often parallels appeals to ethnic support for particular parties. On the other hand, the growing middle class is less engaged in party politics, especially for local assemblies, and that middle class is not driving a change in political campaigning. To explain this phenomenon, Nathan (2019) argues that the middle class has lost confidence in the political process: state capacity is weak and governments fail to credibly commit that they can provide quality public goods. For many in Accra's middle class, when such public services as water or electricity shut off, wealthier citizens turn to their personal water tanks and generators, rather than collectively agitating government for better public services. I would further argue that the iron square of political finance is a key hindrance to government providing quality public goods. Nathan (2019) proposes, amongst other recommendations, that Ghana could deliver programmatic public goods and services through bureaucracies independent of clientelistic practices, similar to reforms that have been introduced in Latin America. Party leaders could implement such reforms when there were clear electoral benefits to doing so.

Donors have frequently recommended the introduction of reforms or isolating local technical experts from clientelistic practices, but the core problems persist. How can those local technical experts be kept free from personal and social pressures? If Nathan (2019) is correct that, despite urbanization, politicians and parties in Africa still use non-programmatic appeals to win votes, then when will it be in parties' favor to introduce and credibly promise programmatic public goods and services? It is not clear that the introduction of such reforms or the rise of an activist middle class would hold in sub-Saharan Africa.

To understand—and contest—why donor and scholarly beliefs that isolating bureaucrats from clientelism or empowering an activist middle class works, it is helpful to refer to the literature on American political machines. Similar to political activities in contemporary Ghana and other developing countries, many American political machines were characterized by ethnic favoritism, graft in procurement, and political-party brokers. Relationships between voters, candidates, and party apparatuses were based on patronage, personal favors, and reciprocal obligations. As such, the historical cases of American political machines are highly relevant to the study of politics in many developing countries. Various scholars have argued that progressive activism and bureaucratic reforms led to the demise of political machines (White 1927; Mowry 1951; Owens, Constantini, & Weschler 1970). Such notions, while important, are likely not sufficient conditions for limiting the power of machines—but these notions can fuel the attribution bias that progressive activism and reforms reduce the power of machines since, in the US, we observe that political machines no longer have the power they once had. This attribution bias can fuel costly, unsuccessful recommendations in developing countries that may not share the same underlying conditions as that the US had decades ago. Donors, who are understandably influenced by their own countries' political histories, should think more deeply about how politics has truly operated. Behind Franklin D. Roosevelt, there was Tammany Hall; behind Harry Truman, Tom Pendergast. The fall of those machines was not solely due to outside reforms and progressive activism. Indeed, such policies may have empowered machines further by giving them access to larger government programs (Katznelson 1981; Boulay & DiGaetano 1985).

The introduction of such reforms, posited by various scholars as explaining the demise of American political machines, does not tell the complete story. While O'Connor (1956) presents the New Deal and its

Federal welfare programs as crowding out the Boston political machine, various authors demonstrate that many city machines actually benefited from the New Deal, which opened up potential patronage and contracting opportunities (Dorsett 1977; Trout 1977; Katznelson 1981). Boulay and DiGaetano (1985) review four types of shifts that contribute to the elimination of American political machines: changes in ethnicity and foreign immigration patterns, municipal reform movements, changes in urban economic structure, and hybrids of these explanations. To test these various hypotheses, Boulay and DiGaetano (1985) examine 33 urban political machines in the US. With respect to changes in ethnicity and foreign immigration, the authors found that in 5 political machines (notably, New York City and Boston) out of the 33, new immigrant groups were able to challenge the established machines and gain control of local government. Progressive urban reform movements managed to dismantle local machines in 10 of the 33 cases, primarily in Western and Midwestern states; however, numerous machines persisted beyond the end of the Progressive era. With respect to changes in urban economic structure, Boulay and DiGaetano (1985) find that in 6 cities out of the 33, changes that led to more diversified or service-oriented economies corresponded with declines in machine power. In many of these cities, suburbanization accompanied economic changes, further diluting the influence of urban machines. Nonetheless, despite these various explanations for the decline of urban political machines, machine politics persisted in Albany and Jersey City until well into the 1970s and 1980s.

There is no all-encompassing theory that explains the downfall of American political machines. As evidenced by the longevity of the Albany and Jersey City machines (amongst others), the argument that Progressive political reforms and new civil-service policies ended political machines encourages attribution bias towards only one reason for the demise of machines. Machines fell for a variety of reasons, including changes in immigration patterns, municipal reforms, shifts in economic structure, and suburbanization. In many cities, these patterns likely worked together, and it is difficult to identify which change is the most significant.

So where does that leave machine politics in a developing country such as Ghana? Ghana is not experiencing suburbanization—rather its urban populations are increasing, but modernization is not necessarily leading to more programmatic politics (Nathan 2019). While the country's growth has improved in recent decades, it is still far from being a wealthy country—Ghana is unlikely to experience the long-term growth and economic shifts that characterized the US economy after World War II, the period in which many machines ended. Unlike the US, Ghana is probably not going to see an influx of immigrants who will upend the existing order.

Without these external factors, how can political leaders in Ghana, who are dependent on the current system, summon the political will to overcome the iron square of political financing and improve the delivery of public goods and services? As shown by Stokes et al. (2013), national political leaders in the US and UK eventually maintained the political will to uphold laws of varying success that eroded machine power. Partly attributable to the urgencies of World War II, the US government oversaw quality improvements in government-procured goods (Nagle 1999). Those emergency conditions do not exist in Ghana to force political leaders to upgrade the procurement of government goods and services. Nonetheless, it will be incumbent upon Ghana's political leaders to change the system from the inside. What role can donors play to generate the political and popular will to improve the provision of public goods and services? Donors will need to go beyond the repeated motif of recommending institutional reforms and think carefully about the underlying uncertainties and norms that govern the system. Donors will need to think creatively and question their own assumptions about "best practices".

Towards localized solutions

As Ghana is unlikely to see in the near future the changes that befell US political machines, change must come from within. In the following paragraphs, I outline a specific recommendation for addressing public procurement challenges and the quality of club- and public-goods delivery in local settings. I then generalize this recommendation to a broader approach to understanding and harnessing political finance in the practice of development.

It is possible that the incentives that define and sustain the iron square can help identify a solution that satisfies players' incentives while also delivering better public goods. For contractors, income uncertainty is a paramount concern. Similar to other cases (Scott 1976; Bates 2001), contractors in Ghana have developed coping devices (subcontracting, side businesses) that help to smooth risks and income uncertainty. It is possible that other players in the ecosystem would prefer stability to the uncertainty that currently accompanies the iron square. Politicians and candidates are likely anxious about rising debts incurred while campaigning. Bureaucrats are concerned about retirement and having a house to settle in. Party chairs worry about supporting their foot soldiers and whether they will be overthrown in the next party elections. These players all draw money from the common resource of local development funds. Is there a way to control extraction from that common resource that benefits all players in the political ecosystem? How can "common knowledge" between the players be improved to help find and sustain a solution?

Such questions fall at the heart of Elinor Ostrom's work on common-pool resources and that work offers guidance towards transcending the iron square. Ostrom (1990) defines a common-pool resource as a natural or man-made resource system that is sufficiently large to make it costly, but not impossible, to exclude potential beneficiaries that are using that resource system. These systems exhibit congestion and then decline when too many extractors are present, e.g., overfishing and deforestation. The development funds that are available to local governments in Ghana resemble a common-pool resource in a variety of ways: they are technically only open to politicians and bureaucrats to "use" (that is, to commit to development projects), but these resources are also being exploited by contractors and party chairs. Further, the number of potential contractors vying for contracts is likely increasing as more foot soldiers see contracts as a source of income, and there is little inspection of contractors' qualifications. As more players place demands on the "flow" of development funds, the "stock" of development funds decreases. Under a tragedy of the commons model, the development funds would disappear in the absence of any control on the demands. Further, there is no guarantee that those demanding the funds would improve the quality of public-goods provision.

Ostrom (1990) empirically demonstrates that there are many cases where local groups have successfully managed common-pool resources. These management arrangements have existed without the need for "extreme" solutions such as privatization or centralized control. Ostrom (1990)'s work draws from diverse, successful cases including land management in Switzerland (Netting 1976) and Japan (McKean 1986) as well as water management in Spain (Glick 1970; Maass & Anderson 1986) and the Philippines (Siy 1982). In these cases, local actors established locally appropriate systems of allocating individual resource use as well as monitoring mechanisms to ensure compliance. In the Japanese case, local household groups were assigned land for extracting winter fodder according to an annual rotation scheme (McKean 1986). In the Spanish case, various communities established a set day of the week where disputes could be heard and adjudicated in public (Glick 1970). In each case, actors found ways to reduce uncertainty around resource extraction; develop monitoring mechanisms; and increase common knowledge about what was forbidden, required, and permitted (Ostrom 1990). From these empirical cases, Ostrom (1990) developed the following eight characteristics of robust common-pool resource management systems:

1   Clearly defined boundaries (of those permitted to extract from the resource)
2   Tailored rules that restrict how potential users can extract from the resource
3   Collective-choice arrangements where those affected by the rules can participate in modifying the rules
4   Monitors that are accountable to those who extract from the resource
5   Graduated sanctions that depend on the seriousness and context of the offense
6   Access to low-cost arenas for resolving conflicts
7   The right of local extractors to devise institutions should not be challenged by external authorities
8   Nested enterprises may be required for management of more complex resources

As constituted, the management of local development funds in Ghana (and their consequent use for political financing) fails many of the criteria listed above. There are no clearly defined boundaries of who may extract from that resource. The current rules—that is, the procurement regulations—are not well enforced. Those affected by the rules have little say in modifying them. And so forth. It is not difficult to posit the many ways in which the management of local funds in developing countries violates Ostrom's (1990) criteria.

Ostrom (1990) and Bates (1988) note that organically creating a new institution to address existing problems is difficult. As Bates (1988) asserts, a proposed new institution "is subject to the very incentive problems it is supposed to resolve". Such an assertion should be relevant for any development practitioner focusing on governance. However, it is critical to remember that such theories as the tragedy of the commons and the iron square of political finance involve people and people can change their ways. Ostrom (1990) argues,

> as long as analysts presume that individuals cannot change such situations themselves, they do not ask what internal or external variables can enhance or impede the efforts of communities of individuals to deal creatively and constructively with perverse problems such as the tragedy of the commons.

I should note that the vast majority of Ghanaian public servants interviewed expressed strong motivation to serve their country. As emphatically stated by one District Chief Executive (DCE),

> I didn't regret serving the people. I served from my heart. Those of us in the [redacted] term—we served from our hearts. I'm not only serving my own (party) people.
>
> Former DCE, party withheld

Development practitioners should recognize that such motivations are not uncommon in developing countries. However, it is critical for practitioners to think about the totality of motivations facing local actors in developing countries and how external interventions can be tailored to unlock and enhance these motivations. Norris and Abel van Es (2016), drawing from various case studies, argue that there is no single right "mix" of political-finance regulations that would suit a diverse array of countries. As demonstrated by Baez Camargo and Koechlin (2018), localized, informal practices shape the ways in which political actors are motivated and engage with each other. Such informal practices likely underpin political-finance practices across many developing countries.

The remainder of this volume seeks to transcend—even break—the iron square. I contend that the formal, sealed-bid procurement rules are inappropriate for local development in developing countries. Formal procurement may have little historical context in developing countries (Toeba 2018), and many modern procurement rules are drawn from the historical relationship between the US government and its military (Nagle 1999). While it is true that sealed-bid procurement may be needed for more complex projects in developing countries, the development-practitioner community should reconsider whether formal procurement is necessary for providing smaller goods and services in local areas. Such sealed-bid procurement introduces uncertainty for contractors and other players—an uncertainty which can be exploited for political gain, as demonstrated by the district tender committee in Chapter 2. That enforced uncertainty is directly at odds with contractors' and other players' desires to reduce income fluctuations to meet their other needs.

In the spirit of Ostrom (1990) and others, I propose changing how procurement is done in the local context of developing countries. The exploitable uncertainty of sealed-bid procurement contributes to the pressures faced by politicians, bureaucrats, contractors, and party chairs to extract funds from local development funds. The goals of changing procurement processes include reducing leakages of funds from projects and improving the quality of projects. Rather than having contractors "bid" for contracts, local politicians, bureaucrats, contractors, and party chairs can work together to:

1 Define a public list of qualified contractors. It is critical for party chairs (of both major parties) to be part of this conversation so that they can ensure that qualified foot soldiers are included.
2 Define a public list of qualified construction-material suppliers. Party chairs can recommend foot soldiers here who might not be qualified to actually build infrastructure.
3 Develop a rotational contract-allocation system. Similar to Ostrom's (1990) empirical descriptions of common-pool resources, in a given year, contractors can be guaranteed a publicly known order in which they select contracts to build. That order would then be changed in the following year, depending on local circumstances and monitoring mechanisms. As a result, contractors can have more certainty about when they—and others—will receive a contract.[1]
4 Develop a monitoring system to ensure that contractors do not cut corners. Since it will be common knowledge that party chairs recommended particular contractors, they will have incentive to ensure that "their" contractors do quality work.
5 Develop a public system of dispute resolution and amendment of these rules. For instance, weekly town meetings could be held at the local chief's palace. As traditional leaders, chiefs may be especially effective at resolving disputes, perhaps by reinforcing kinship ties between litigants.
6 Develop rules for periodically revising lists of qualified contractors and suppliers. For instance, these lists could be revised every four years, but in between each national election. As such, party chairs may be more willing to cooperate with opposition chairs on list selection since there may be a party change in government and they may be working with opposition politicians.

Such a system addresses several of Ostrom's (1990) criteria to help reduce uncertainty concerning the common resource of local-development funds. Defining public lists of contractors and suppliers helps to create boundaries on who is allowed to extract from local development funds. Though it may seem controversial to include party chairs in selecting contractors and suppliers, it is an open secret in Ghana that political parties influence contracts. The rotational contract-allocation system sets appropriate restrictions on when contractors can extract from the funds, i.e., they can only select a contract to build when it is their turn in the rotation.

While it is possible that in some local contexts, local players will be able to self-monitor, monitoring is an area where donor assistance might be valuable. Such monitoring could include ensuring project quality, but also facilitating selection of qualified-contractor lists and helping local authorities—both formal and traditional—adjudicate disputes. Ostrom (1990) describes an irrigation-management project in Sri Lanka in which institutional organizers—"catalysts"—were introduced to listen to farmers' needs and help them organize and develop self-help strategies. Such catalysts improved farmer coordination and relations with local officials. In the case of monitoring, donors could provide monitors directly (i.e., through donor-sponsored volunteer programs or in partnership with a recipient country's volunteer program, such as Ghana's National Service) or provide financial incentives for local monitors who perform quality work.

To ease monitoring for project quality, donor-funded projects could emphasize simpler, more locally appropriate materials, technologies, and labor (Schumacher 1973). Donors should consider carefully the desire to apply "best practices" or the newest technologies to solve local club- and public-good problems. Those practices or technologies may not be appropriate for a local development context, and may be more difficult for local citizens to maintain in the long term. "Appropriate technology" could also help to lower costs, both for initial building and long-term maintenance. For example, in construction, local earth materials may be more appropriate for building schools and market stalls than cement, which often requires capital equipment. Such materials can be sourced locally and may require less expertise to use compared to cement, potentially expanding the pool of labor that could benefit from working on such a project. The use of locally appropriate technologies also allows for more effective monitoring by local authorities (since less technical expertise may be required) and citizens.

While removing procurement-related uncertainty is a necessary condition for improving management of local development funds, it is not sufficient, given that players will still be facing outside pressures. Bureaucrats may be relieved to avoid the ethical dilemmas of tender-committee meetings, and they may have more time to do their actual jobs, such as inspecting projects, but they will likely still face pressures to save for retirement and build a house. Bureaucrats need to trust that the pension system will support them once they reach retirement age. Donors could work with recipient central governments to better manage pension systems to guarantee bureaucrats a reasonable retirement—thereby reducing uncertainty in the present day. Donors could further work with central governments to provide retirement housing subsidies for bureaucrats to help retirees build, purchase, or rent a home. To provide additional incentive for bureaucrats to do quality work, such housing subsidies could be tied to their performance, as monitored by local actors.

Politicians will continue to face pressure from constituents for funds to pay for hospital fees, school tuition, funerals, etc. It is possible that with local contractors and suppliers being guaranteed contract opportunities requests will diminish as constituents can borrow from members of their kin group. However, such requests will likely still come, and politicians will not have enough funds to pay them out of pocket. Donors could help provide such assistance funds for local governments, but donor-sponsored monitors could also facilitate informal (or formal) contracts between politicians and constituents requesting money: if a constituent receives direct financial assistance from a politician, then she could publicly commit to perform an appropriate kind of community service, such as cleanup of public facilities. Such a contract mechanism could help to reduce requests for money while also providing valuable community service.

Perhaps more critically, politicians will continue to face pressures to finance their campaigns. Under the proposed system of public, rotational contracting, such financing may be easier or more difficult to obtain. Campaign financing, however, resembles an arms race: spending more than your opponent(s) can increase your chance of winning. However, is it possible for candidates to agree, before primaries and general elections, not to exceed some set spending limit? Could campaign funds be kept in escrow and publicly monitored, perhaps in cooperation with banks? Could donors incentivize citizens to report candidates' violations of funding constraints? While such an agreement may be difficult to monitor at a national level, it may be easier to enforce at the level of a parliamentary constituency. Local governments could also agree to provide candidates with appropriate, free fora in which to debate and hold rallies. These are questions that could be explored by donors and their monitors and volunteers. It is possible that many candidates and parties would rather not spend huge sums of money, realizing that such behavior leads to an arms race and more financial pressure. Party chairs, in particular, may be interested in reducing the obligations they must pay to current and prospective foot soldiers. Reducing such financial obligations may open the door to more highly qualified candidates. What might politics and development look like if political decision makers were indebted to no one?

Antiheroes and Machine-Guided Development

The preceding paragraphs address how donors and local-development partners can tackle the corruption and poor quality associated with formal procurement. But, without exogenous economic growth or an activist urban middle class, how can political machines ultimately break free of the iron square and provide higher quality public goods? How can it be in their interest?

I propose that donors adopt a mindset of Machine-Guided Development. That is, donors (and scholars) should not think of political machines as mere obstacles to be reformed. After all, political machines do identify and resolve some of the private needs of citizens, needs that are not being met by programmatic policies. This is not to say that machines and their leaders are benevolent charities. As I demonstrate in this book, machines do engage in corruption and favoritism, activities that impose costs on the public. But machines also understand their voters.

There is a tendency to conflate reformers with heroes. In primarily recommending policy reforms or bureaucracies isolated from clientelism, donors are implicitly advancing the claim that more heroes are needed in development, that those who change the system must be brave, selfless, and fighting for good. In the US, the Progressive reform movement did play important roles in improving the quality of life in urban areas, but they were not the sole cause of such improvements. Changes in economic and demographic structures also helped to undermine the power of urban machines and shift non-programmatic policies to the programmatic provision of public goods (Boulay & DiGaetano 1985). Heroes were not solely responsible for political development in developed countries. On the other hand, many see political-party chairs and those politicians, bureaucrats, and contractors entwined in corruption as villains, seeking only to enrich themselves.

I argue that those politicians, bureaucrats, contractors, and political-party chairs can be better characterized as antiheroes. They are not heroes in that they do engage in activities for self-interested reasons: politicians need money to win election campaigns, bureaucrats are saving for retirement, contractors are seeking stable revenues, and party chairs are serving their loyal party supporters. But they are not villains who do not care for the public good or the welfare of others.

> What I achieved was my joy. I didn't go [into party politics] for self. I went to serve people and win power for my party. It's a game that I enjoy. Politics made me rich in experience—so much! ... I know how my Ghanaians feel in all aspects of life. I'm thankful for politics.
>
> Former NDC Regional Chair, Coastal Zone

Many of the politicians, bureaucrats, contractors, and political-party chairs in my sample went into politics and administration with noble goals. They wanted to serve their fellow Ghanaians. However, they were compromised by a system of political financing and forced to play games to survive in the system. In the iron square, each of these players is playing ultimatum games. If a contractor wants a contract, she must give 10% of the funds to a bureaucrat so that the bureaucrat can approve the contract. If a bureaucrat wants funds for retirement, she must condone a politician's illicit activities. If a politician wants to win reelection to carry out her agenda, she must provide funds to the party chair. If the chair wants to keep serving his people, he must extract funds from procurement. All of these ultimatum games are framed by collective-action problems and social norms that sustain the system and discourage individuals from speaking out against the system—that is, from being heroes. Many of these actors, despite their heroic inclinations, are compromised by the system and must act selfishly or short-sightedly, thereby making then antiheroes.

How can donors bring out the heroic tendencies of these development antiheroes? In applying Ostrom's (1990) principles of common-pool resources to procurement, I aimed to reduce uncertainty for the various players. For contractors, it was not clear when they would ever receive contracts; consequently, there were uncertain funding streams for politicians, bureaucrats, and party chairs, all of whom depend on procurement contracts to meet their needs. Such uncertainty allows the ultimatum games that these players play to thrive. If parties and contractors have predictability as to when contracts will arrive, then they can plan around those expected revenue streams. As such, the ultimatum games between the players start to weaken—players do not need to bribe each other to ensure a contractor gets a contract. They can rather wait for that contractor's turn for a contract, which is public knowledge. Of course, it is not sufficient to just make such ultimatum games more predictable. There needs to be enforcement to ensure project quality is upheld. It is possible that donors and local players could facilitate project monitoring—if party chairs have a stake, they could oversee their foot soldiers to ensure that they construct according to quality standards.

For donors, it is key to identify the main interests and uncertainties facing politicians, bureaucrats, and other players in a developing country—specifically, the uncertainties around how these players raise money to sustain such activities as elections, future planning, and so forth. Elections are obviously critical to politicians: they need to win them to stay in power. For bureaucrats, most of whom live on low salaries but face mandatory retirement ages, how do they save for their futures? In other developing countries besides Ghana, there may be different uncertainties, but it is still likely that political and bureaucratic players there will need to raise money to meet those needs.

Beyond politicians and bureaucrats, it is crucial to understand the interests of local political-party leaders—that is, those who are intimately involved with machine politics. While externally most would profess that their key interest is to defeat the other party or parties in elections, in reality many such leaders work to serve their constituents. It is not always the case that they are in perpetual competition with the other parties.

> With the NDC it was quite cordial. Only in public would there be radio antagonism. Apart from that, it was cordial. We were going to each other's funerals. In Ghana, funeral attendance goes a long way. Anyone who goes to a funeral hasn't got anything against you.
>
> Former NPP Regional Chair, Coastal Zone

Though many such regional chairs may enjoy the hustle and bustle of the political game and striking deals for their supporters, many would also admit that such a game is exhausting and stressful, filled with intrigue and internal strife. For these chairs, it is likely exhausting to always be looking for contracting and job opportunities for their supporters. They likely have many other formal and informal duties to fulfill, and political-economy analysts should map out the various demands that chairs face. Is it possible that machine leaders might prefer to work together to provide quality public goods and services to their constituents? What prevents them from doing so?

After identifying interests and uncertainties, donors' political-economy analysts should find ways to ask how these different players raise the money to meet their needs. In developed countries today, salaries and personal investments may suffice, but that is likely not the case in developing countries with low salaries and a weak investment market. Though it may seem daunting to ascertain how politicians, bureaucrats, contractors, and chairs raise funds, especially through corrupt procurement practices, they may be entirely forthcoming—which would not be surprising for antiheroes with fundamentally good intentions. Further, in Ghana, procurement-based corruption is an open secret. Citizens and chiefs in local areas knew that it occurred—possibly because many of them subsequently benefited from this corruption. In other countries, these players may have different methods for raising additional money, ranging from petty corruption to gifts and so forth.

Once interests and sources of funding have been identified, political-economy analysts should consider the networks in which such interests and funds extraction operate. Who relies on whom? Who enforces what? What is the actual flow of money between players? Depending on the structure of local governments, bureaucracies, party systems, and local power brokers, development's antiheroes may have extensive networks on which they must rely to meet their needs. The iron square may have more or fewer sides, more or fewer links between each player. In local development settings, these players may be very close to each other, with daily interactions.

Lastly, political-economy analysts should delve into the reasons why such interactions are sustained. Why do potential reformers, especially respected religious and traditional leaders, not speak up? Why do such interactions persist, even when there are changes in government or leadership? As identified in this book, many of these interactions are sustained by collective-action problems. Bureaucrats are hesitant to challenge politicians on corruption because they will need that politician in the future. A region's politicians are unable to coordinate to challenge a chair on corruption because there are strong incentives to defect. Such persistence may be couched in deep social norms—reciprocity and risk aversion, in particular. These norms may run counter to what we expect in politics. For instance, seemingly acrimonious political parties may actually work together to ensure their mutual survival. With many players, these interactions are simply personal rather than adversarial. Of course, there may indeed be enmity between certain players, but political-economy analysts should not assume that such enmity is the default scenario. As political-economy analysts map out this system they can identify areas where donors can help local partners to reduce uncertainty (or, more specifically, to stabilize revenue expectations of each player) so that interactions based on ultimatum games can become more cooperative and less costly. Stabilizing such revenue expectations of these key decision makers can help local development's antiheroes start to look beyond merely surviving and meeting their needs to ensuring quality delivery of local goods and services.

The goal of Machine-Guided Development is to work with machines—and the social system in which they are encased—to improve public-goods delivery and ultimately put the non-programmatic (i.e., costly, inefficient provision of private goods) aspects of machines out of business. Many party chairs in my sample want to see schools and hospitals built; they want their constituents to have better access to education, healthcare, and various other areas. If donors can help machines to overcome the ultimatum games, collective-action problems, and social norms that negatively impact public-goods delivery, then maybe machines can deliver those goods to a higher quality. If machines can do that, then voters—especially in the middle class—can start to gain confidence in state capacity in developing countries. It is possible, then, that voters, politicians, and even machines will be ready to address larger questions of programmatic delivery of public goods and services. Donors can help the political and bureaucratic players to credit claim such successes. It may seem unnatural to think that machine leaders and those that benefit from corruption would be willing to deliver quality public goods—but political-economy analysts should not assume such a negative position towards these actors. They are not necessarily villains, but perhaps one-time heroes changed by the circumstances of their world into antiheroes. Donors can help these players to reshape those circumstances. As Elinor Ostrom (2009) said,

> ...humans have a more complex motivational structure and more capability to solve social dilemmas than posited in earlier rational-choice theory. Designing institutions to force (or nudge) entirely self-interested individuals to achieve better outcomes has been the major goal posited by policy analysts for governments to accomplish for much of the past half century. Extensive empirical research leads me to argue that instead, a core goal of public policy should be to facilitate the development of institutions that bring out the best in humans.

Future research

This book is one attempt to catalog, in depth, how politics is financed in a single developing country. It is likely not even a complete picture of how politics is financed in Ghana. While I assert that this book illuminates common themes that will apply to other developing countries, there is a need to collect qualitative and quantitative data that answers the question: how is politics actually financed? There is growing data on political-finance regulations around the world (Norris and Abel van Es 2016), but little clear understanding of the sources of money in politics. In many countries, this topic touches on sensitive areas, and it is not the kind of topic where data is readily available. Donors should consider sponsoring undergraduates, graduate students, and faculty across the social sciences to start chipping away at understanding where the money for political activities in these countries comes from.

As such research is being conducted, I also recommend that political-economy analysts start building a database of political machines and power brokers in developing countries. In two-party states like Ghana, this might be easier where there is a relatively well-defined number of parties and some semblance of institutionalized structure in these parties. However, such a task is likely more difficult in countries with proportional-representation systems, where there may be a multitude of parties and power brokers, many of whom would be more difficult to track down. Nonetheless, donors and scholars should catalog these machines and interview their leaders and supporters. What are their incentives? What are the challenges that these machines face? What development outcomes would they like to see their people realize?

Political-economy analysts and scholars should also gather data on the needs and incentives of bureaucrats in developing countries. I was surprised by the extent to which bureaucrats all across my sample listed retirement concerns as their top priority while in the civil service—these concerns drove bureaucrats to condone and partake in procurement corruption. In Ghana, such concerns also extended to what kind of housing bureaucrats would have upon retirement. Donors could assist partner countries with developing a robust pension system for public servants along with increasing availability of modest housing that could be sold or rented to retired public servants. It is likely that such concerns are prevalent for bureaucrats in other countries and that there are additional concerns that bureaucrats may be facing. Donors are starting to pay closer attention to bureaucrats, as evidenced by the establishment of the World Bank's Bureaucracy Lab.

Donors should also better understand the needs and incentives of contractors that actually build projects or supply services in developing countries. Contractors desire revenue stability, but promoting systems of formal procurement may have the inequitable effects of favoring wealthier contractors and those with connections. Many contractors are hesitant to merge or formally pool their resources to provide better services because of individual incentives to save money for their own families. Donors, as expected, want contractors who are selected to perform jobs to be of higher quality, but donors should assess whether there are constraints to contractors investing in themselves. As noted in this book, contractors may be undertaking side businesses or subcontracting due to social norms and a need to survive in the long term. Donors should consider whether there are ways to alleviate those burdens.

Beyond these actors, scholars and practitioners should study innovative ways in which formal rules can be adapted to fit local contexts better. The recommended changes to formal procurement above represent one such reformulation of an institution that has facilitated corruption. Initiatives such as Global Integrity's Anti-Corruption Evidence Research Programme are studying new ways to understand corruption, and current research activities are exploring how informal practices can be harnessed to enhance social accountability and local anti-corruption efforts (Basel Institute on Governance 2019; Global Integrity 2019).

Conclusion

It is time for development practitioners to think about how political finance influences development outcomes. In Ghana, such political funds are intertwined with sealed-bid procurement processes that are mandated at the local levels. Are such processes really necessary? Can those processes ever be adapted and aligned with realities on the ground? I argue that sealed-bid procurement is incompatible with the realities facing impoverished local governments in developing countries. The players within this political ecosystem face much income uncertainty, and they wish to reduce that uncertainty. As currently constituted, the political ecosystem for managing local-development funds is bound in an iron square of ultimatum games, with players' exploitation of funds serving personal interests without improving development outcomes. The players' behaviors are further constrained by collective-action problems—discouraging individuals from pushing reforms—and social norms that prioritize reciprocity for future assistance.

The players involved in this iron square, however, are not necessarily villains. Consequently, donors should be careful of prescribing development solutions that are better suited for heroes or ideal circumstances. Rather, the iron square of political finance has caused the politicians, bureaucrats, contractors, and party chairs in Ghana to deviate from heroic intentions towards acting as antiheroes. These players want to survive and be able to deliver benefits to themselves, their extended networks, and to Ghanaians overall. They have public goals that they would like to meet, whether it is providing better education, transportation, healthcare, and so forth. But no player has hope of meeting those goals if they do not play the games that must be played to stay in the political sphere.

However, it is possible for the political ecosystem to be better managed: donors can work with local partners to change formal procurement processes and develop locally appropriate rules and monitoring. Such rules can reduce uncertainty and stabilize revenues for the partners involved by disempowering the ultimatum games that are played between the players. When ultimatums are replaced by predictable, stable revenues, players may act more in accord with the public interest, potentially delivering better public goods and services for citizens. There are many development practitioners and local partners who are committed to reducing corruption and improving livelihoods. It is possible that, under the right circumstances, political machines can provide better public goods and services, ultimately putting their non-programmatic operations out of business. Despite pollution and leakage of its resources, the political ecosystem can recover, thrive, and deliver better outcomes to the public.

Note

1 Some Ghanaian contractors that receive contracts from local politicians have created a rotational system: in a few of the districts in my sample, the same three contractors would bid for a series of projects, but a different contractor would provide the lowest qualified bid for a given project and win. Blundo and Olivier de Sardan (2007) describe similar "tontines" occurring between contractors in French West Africa. However, these rotational systems only benefit the contractors within them (who might not have been qualified contractors) and are still associated with kickbacks and poor construction quality.

References

Apter, David. 1965. *The Politics of Modernization*. Chicago, IL: University of Chicago Press.

Baez Camargo, Claudia and Lucy Koechlin. 2018. "Informal Governance: Comparative Perspectives on Co-optation, Control, and Camouflage in Rwanda, Tanzania and Uganda." *International Development Policy*, 10: 78–100.

Basel Institute on Governance. 2019. "Harnessing Informality to Promote Integrity and Design Better Anti-Corruption Programmes—New Research Project." URL: https://www.baselgovernance.org/news/harnessing-informality-promote-integrity-and-design-better-anti-corruption-programmes-new

Bates, Robert. 1988. "Contra Contractarianism: Some Reflections on the New Institutionalism." *Politics and Society*, 16(2): 387–401.

Bates, Robert. 2001. *Prosperity and Violence: The Political Economy of Development*. New York, NY: W.W. Norton.

Blundo, Giorgio and Jean-Pierre Olivier de Sardan. 2006. *Everyday Corruption and the State*. London: Zed Books.

Boulay, Harvey and Alan DiGaetano. 1985. "Why Did Political Machines Disappear?" *Journal of Urban History*, 12(1): 25–49.

Carothers, Thomas and Diane De Gramont. 2013. *Development Aid Confronts Politics: The Almost Revolution*. Washington, DC: Carnegie Endowment for International Peace.

Dorsett, Lyle. 1977. *Franklin Roosevelt and the City Bosses*. Port Washington, NY: Kennikat Press.

Glick, Thomas. 1970. *Irrigation and Society in Medieval Valencia*. Cambridge, MA: Harvard University Press.

Global Integrity. 2019. "Global Integrity Anti-Corruption Evidence Programme (GI-ACE)." URL: https://www.globalintegrity.org/ace/

Katznelzon, Ira. 1981. *City Trenches*. Chicago, IL: University of Chicago Press.

Maass, Arthur and Raymond Anderson. 1986. *And the Desert Shall Rejoice: Conflict, Growth, and Justice in Arid Environments*. Malabar, FL: R.E. Krieger.

Lessig, Lawrence. 2011. *Republic, Lost: How Money Corrupts Congress—And a Plan to Stop It*. New York, NY: Twelve.

Lipset, Seymour Martin. 1960. *Political Man: The Social Bases of Politics*. New York. NY: Doubleday.

McKean, Margaret. 1986. "Management of Traditional Common Lands (Iriaichi) in Japan." In *Proceedings of the Conference on Common Property Resource Management*, National Research Council. Washington, DC: National Academy Press.

Mowry, George. 1951. *The California Progressives*. Berkeley: University of California Press.

Nagle, James. 1999. *A History of Government Contracting, Second Edition*. Washington, DC: The George Washington University.

Nathan, Noah. 2019. *Electoral Politics and Africa's Urban Transition: Class and Ethnicity in Ghana*. Cambridge, UK: Cambridge University Press.

Netting, Robert McC. 1976. "What Alpine Peasants Have in Common: Observations on Communal Tenure in a Swiss Village." *Human Ecology*, 4(2): 135–146.

Norris, Pippa and Andrea Abel van Es, ed. 2016. *Checkbook Elections? Political Finance in Comparative Perspective*. Oxford, UK: Oxford University Press.

O'Connor, Edwin. 1956. *The Last Hurrah*. Boston, MA: Little, Brown.

Ostrom, Elinor. 1990. *Governing the Commons: The Evolution of Institutions for Collective Action*. Cambridge, UK: Cambridge University Press.

Ostrom, Elinor. 2009. "Beyond Markets and States: Polycentric Governance of Complex Economic Systems." Nobel Prize Lecture.

Owens, John, Edmond Constantini, and Louis Weschler. 1970. *California Politics and Parties*. London, UK: MacMillan.

Schumacher, Ernst. 1973. *Small Is Beautiful: A Study of Economics as If People Mattered.* London, UK: Blond & Briggs.

Scott, James. 1976. *The Moral Economy of the Peasant: Rebellion and Subsistence in Southeast Asia.* New Haven, CT: Yale University Press.

Siy, Robert, Jr. 1982. *Community Resource Management: Lessons from the Zanjera.* Quezon City: University of the Philippines Press.

Stokes, Susan, Thad Dunning, Marcelo Nazareno, and Valeria Brusco. 2013. *Brokers, Voters, and Clientelism: The Puzzle of Distributive Politics.* Cambridge, UK: Cambridge University Press.

Toeba, Thato. 2018. "Corruption in Public Procurement in Lesotho." *The Law and Development Review,* 11(2): 397–431.

Trout, Charles. 1977. *Boston: The Great Depression and the New Deal.* New York, NY: Oxford University Press.

White, Leonard. 1927. *The City Manager.* Chicago, IL: The University of Chicago Press.

Index

For Product Safety Concerns and Information please contact our EU
representative GPSR@taylorandfrancis.com
Taylor & Francis Verlag GmbH, Kaufingerstraße 24, 80331 München, Germany

www.ingramcontent.com/pod-product-compliance
Lightning Source LLC
Chambersburg PA
CBHW050536270326
41926CB00015B/3251